THERE IS LIFE AFTER COLLEGE

"This book is an important wake-up call for anyone concerned with the future of our higher-education system, as well as an invaluable guide for students who want to make the most of their college years."   —Paul Tough, *New York Times* bestselling author of *How Children Succeed*

"Features many valuable stories from his interviews with students who figure out how to thrive in various career trajectories."
—*The Atlantic*

"Selingo provides an important road map for navigating the world of higher education. This is an essential guide for learning what to expect from college, and how to prepare for productive employment afterward."
—Janet Napolitano, president of the University of California, former secretary of Homeland Security, and former governor of Arizona

"Selingo provides valuable and practical information about what kids *really* need to know to not just be employable, but to be in a position to know what they want, know how to get there, and succeed once they've arrived."
—Jessica Lahey, *New York Times* bestselling author of *The Gift of Failure*

"Explores several promising experiments that promise to redefine college as we know it."   —*USA Today*

"A necessary and thoughtful contribution to the conversation on the role our colleges and universities play in preparing students for young adulthood. Everyone who has an interest in the development of today's college students and tomorrow's leaders should read it."
—Dan Porterfield, President of Franklin and Marshall College

"Drawing upon his decades of research and extensive conversations with twentysomethings, educators, and employers, Selingo convincingly frames the twenty-first-century job market

as a wholly unfamiliar terrain, then provides comprehensive strategies and tactical tips for tackling it."
—Julie Lythcott-Haims, author of *How to Raise an Adult*

"Selingo demonstrates the radical changes complicating young people's transitions to adulthood; highlights emerging and necessary transformations in the delivery of higher education; and at the same time, gives students and their parents practical guidance in charting the best course."
—Hilary Pennington, Ford Foundation Vice President for Education, Creativity, and Free Expression

"Levelheaded advice for students and parents on the best path to take from high school to employment."   —*Kirkus Reviews*

"*There Is Life After College* is essential reading for high school and college students and their parents. Selingo weaves the stories of numerous young graduates throughout a narrative replete with useful tips for those who are facing the future. Students looking for a road map to the future should get this book and heed its advice."   —Patricia Rose, Director of Career Services, University of Pennsylvania

"In an age when jobs and career paths are likely to shift—and even evaporate entirely—at an unprecedented pace, Jeffrey Selingo's *There Is Life After College* offers a practical road map for graduates faced with navigating a challenging and unpredictable terrain."   —Martin Ford, author of *Rise of the Robots: Technology and the Threat of a Jobless Future*

"Bursting with fresh ideas and vivid examples. . . . The breadth and depth of Selingo's expertise make him a uniquely good guide to what's undeniably a complicated topic."
—EdSurge.com

"*There Is Life After College* is a must-read for high-school students, those in college, recent graduates and their parents."
—Edward B. Rust, Jr., Chairman of the Board, State Farm Mutual Automobile Insurance Company

THERE IS LIFE AFTER COLLEGE

What Parents and Students Should Know
About Navigating School to Prepare for the
Jobs of Tomorrow

Jeffrey J. Selingo

WILLIAM MORROW
An Imprint of HarperCollins*Publishers*

HarperCollins books may be purchased for educational, business, or sales promotional use. For information please e-mail the Special Markets Department at SPsales@harpercollins.com.

A hardcover edition of this book was published in 2016 by William Morrow, an imprint of HarperCollins Publishers.

FIRST WILLIAM MORROW PAPERBACK EDITION PUBLISHED 2017.

Library of Congress Cataloging-in-Publication Data has been applied for.

ISBN 978-0-06-238885-8

17 18 19 20 21   OV/LSC   10 9 8 7 6 5 4 3 2 1

For Hadley, Rory, and Heather,
who are a constant source of inspiration for my stories

CONTENTS

INTRODUCTION

NOT SO LONG AGO A NEWLY MINTED COLLEGE DEGREE WAS THE TICKET TO A SOLID FIRST JOB AFTER GRADUATION, FOLLOWED BY A SUCCESSful career. Any anxiety that parents and their teenage children felt about going off to college was largely limited to the front end of the process: getting into a good school, figuring out how to pay the tuition bill, choosing the right major.

Rarely were students or their parents concerned that college wouldn't supply them with the knowledge and skills needed to survive in the work world—all that mattered was undergraduates emerged on the other side with some sort of credential. A degree was an easily recognizable signal to employers of potential and discipline, one that grew stronger the more selective the school on the résumé.

But today there seems to be a lot of noise interfering with that signal. At the same time that more and more people are earning a bachelor's degree, employers are trusting less and less that it is an indicator of real job readiness. As a result, a college senior no longer has as clear or straightforward a career path as previous generations did.

It's easy to blame the job struggles college graduates have been having on the lackluster economic recovery in recent years. But the plight of today's young adults is not confined to one single moment in the economic cycle. Rather it is a result of a longer-term shift in the global workforce that is having an outsized impact on people in their twenties who have little work experience.

Recently, unemployment among the young has risen to highs not seen in four decades, at one point reaching an alarming 9 percent for recent college graduates under the age of twenty-five. For those who found jobs, the average wage of workers with a bachelor's degree has declined 10 percent in the first part of this century.

Perhaps more disturbing is that nearly half of college graduates in their twenties are underemployed, meaning the jobs they can get don't require a bachelor's degree. "Having a B.A. is less about obtaining access to high-paying managerial and technology jobs and more about beating out less-educated workers for the barista and clerical job" was the conclusion of a widely cited report by three economists in 2014. That study also found demand for college-educated knowledge workers has slowed as the tech revolution has matured. In other words, the stereotype of the college graduate working at Starbucks or as a waiter is no exaggeration. And it suggested that this situation may be the new normal—where a bachelor's degree is needed to get *any* job, not just a high-skilled, high-wage job.

In 2013, soon after I published a book on the future of

higher education called *College (Un)bound,* I met many of these recent graduates who were struggling to launch into a career. As I crisscrossed the country talking about the college of tomorrow, young adults told me how they were moving from internship to internship without ever finding full-time work. Parents asked me what their kids who had just graduated from college without getting a full-time job had done wrong. High school guidance counselors wondered what advice they should give to students considering college.

Everyone wanted to know if there were other paths to a successful life beyond the one suggested to most teenagers: graduate from high school, go straight to college three months later (preferably a four-year one), and get a job. If colleges were undergoing massive changes, were there new pathways emerging to prepare for a career and land those crucial first jobs in life?

In this book I set out to answer their questions. How can young adults navigate the route from high school through college and into an increasingly perilous economy? What are the fundamental experiences that shape their success in the job market? What skills prove most helpful? And most of all, why do some prosper while others fail?

To begin to find the answers, I took a train trip with some two dozen recent college graduates who were asking many of the same questions themselves.

The mid-August sun was just beginning to set as Amtrak's Capitol Limited set out from Chicago's Union Station. Within minutes, the eastbound train was rolling through the mostly shuttered steel yards of Gary, Indiana. At the rear of the train, in a chartered 1950s-era glass-domed dining car, I was sitting with a group of new college graduates, soaking up the last moments of daylight.

"This is home to U.S. Steel's Gary Works," someone in the back corner of the car shouted out. "It used to be the world's largest steel mill."

A few of the passengers glanced up briefly at the relic of their grandparents' generation, who worked at a time when the American economy was fueled by factories and when the pathway through a career was simple and linear: graduate from high school or college; get a good job with advancement opportunities, training programs, and a pension; work thirty-odd years and then retire.

The group I was traveling with—born mostly in the late 1980s—is part of a much more complex, fragmented workforce with many overlapping pathways. While their grandparents, and even their parents, had maps with clearly marked trails for their careers, this generation faces wide-open seas as they chart their next thirty-plus years.

This was day eight of the Millennial Trains Project, a cross-country rail trip for two dozen twentysomethings, each of whom pitched a real-world project to explore while they traveled from San Francisco to Washington, D.C. In daylong stops along the way—Denver, Omaha, Chicago—they conducted research in local communities, and as they traveled by night, they heard from guest lecturers who hopped on board the train for an overnight journey.

Think of it as one intense, mostly sleepless, but fun week of college for a group of young people trying to figure out how they wanted to live their lives.

As darkness descended over the Indiana farmlands and dinner was served, Cameron Hardesty and Jessica Straus slid into the cramped booth across from me. The pair of chatty twenty-six-year-olds told me they had graduated in 2007 with degrees in English from Davidson College, a well-regarded liberal arts college just north of Charlotte, North Carolina.

Davidson is the kind of small school that prides itself on providing students with broad foundational skills, but it is not a place that trains you for a narrowly tailored job. You can't major in sports management, physical therapy, or video game design at Davidson, for instance. I asked Cameron and Jessica what they thought of their undergraduate experience.

"It didn't prepare me at all for the real world," Jessica said somewhat abruptly.

While she had fond memories of Davidson for allowing her to pursue her dreams—study in Cambridge, work at an art gallery in Barcelona—she said her courses didn't encourage her to translate classroom learning into the explicit know-how sought by employers today. "It was very permissible at Davidson to just explore," she said.

Exploration, of course, was what college used to be: the informative stage between adolescence and adulthood. The training for employment we now seem to expect of colleges and universities came later, either in graduate school or on the job. But today, with the cost of college approaching $240,000 for four years on a campus like Davidson, students (and their parents) demand a set of specific skills that can land them a job at graduation. They still want the broad education—critical thinking, writing and communication, and analytical reasoning—as long as it doesn't come at the expense of outside-the-classroom, hands-on experiences, particularly internships.

Exploration for its own sake in college is now just a slice of the overall experience, and a shrinking slice at that. Within months, even weeks, of arriving on campus, college freshmen are expected to settle on a major (or maybe even two), add a minor, and begin lining up internships that increasingly are required for the best jobs after graduation.

I was on board the Capitol Limited to give a talk about the future of higher education. It was now approaching midnight, and my two seatmates seemed to be catching their second wind. They realized they were among a pretty privileged bunch. They were all on the train because each raised $5,000 as part of a competitive application process. Many of them, like Cameron and Jessica, had also graduated from elite, selective colleges.

They were smart and ambitious, and that's what worried me: If these recent graduates were struggling, what about those who didn't have their pedigrees?

Our conversation turned to the value of the bachelor's degree in an age when everyone they knew had one. Cameron and Jessica told me about classmates and friends working odd jobs in New York City as executive assistants.

"The college degree is becoming the new high school diploma," Cameron remarked.

She is part of a generation that followed what they were told was *the* pathway to solid jobs and careers. They jumped through all the right hoops: aced college-prep classes in high school, earned high scores on the SAT, and, most of all, won the admissions lottery that landed them at a choice college. Once there, they continued to burnish their résumés with what they considered the right markers: double majors, multiple internships, and a slew of extracurricular activities.

But they are also a generation raised by hovering helicopter parents, who scheduled every moment of their free time with playdates and travel soccer teams. Then they arrived on college campuses where a slew of advisers helped them with everything from picking classes so they would graduate on time to negotiating problems with roommates.

No wonder employers complain that recent college graduates are unable to make independent decisions on the job. For many twentysomethings, life to this point has been like a board game, the goal being to get to the end quickly while picking up as many game pieces as possible.

Of course, only a few top prizes are even available. Most twentysomethings don't end up with their dream job after graduation. Many remain adrift and encounter numerous bumps in their transition to a career. Just three days earlier, while the Millennial Trains Project was stopped in Denver, Jessica learned she had been laid off from her job at a tech start-up in New York. She had been there only seven months. Now she was another statistic, another unemployed twentysomething.

This book got its start that August night as I rode the rails from Chicago to Pittsburgh. In the following months, while reporting this book, I found many new college graduates drifting through their twenties without a plan.

One out of four people in their twenties takes an unpaid job simply to show they have work experience, and only one out of ten considers their current job a career. Recent college graduates are starting their careers much later and are delaying the traditional markers of adulthood: completing school, leaving home, getting married, and having children.

A survey of 750 young adults that I commissioned for this book found that two out of three don't launch immediately from any form of post–high school education. Faced with unemployment or temp jobs with low wages in a "gig economy," many young adults are returning home after college to live in their parents' basement, earning the moniker "the boomerang generation."

If you're a parent desperately waiting for your kids to graduate from college so you won't have to support them financially anymore, think again. Maybe you're a child of the 1970s and 1980s, when college graduates, on average, reached financial independence by the time they turned twenty-six years old. Today, college graduates don't hit that mark until their thirtieth birthday.

Teenagers and young adults have many hurdles in front of them on their way to a fulfilling life once they graduate from high school and college, and they need to actively manage their course to a career.

This book will help you get off to the right start on that journey. What it won't do, though, is set out a single path or another set of hoops for twentysomethings. This is about shifting how we think about life after college, about the trajectory toward a successful career—a journey that is not linear, but personal and unique.

Over the course of the chapters ahead, I'll describe a broad range of approaches for students to follow and programs to discover—both while they are in college and after they are out—that are already helping college graduates land firmly on their feet.

The employment statistics about recent college graduates are certainly disturbing, maybe even downright scary, but as I'll outline in Chapter 1, the runway to adulthood and a career has been getting longer for several decades, and for good reason. One out of every three children born today might live to see their hundredth birthday. We're living longer and working longer.

Imagine a timeline of your life, with birth on the left and death on the right: our working careers are shifting to the right—we're starting later and ending later. That shift is allowing younger people extended periods in their teens and twenties to explore options for careers and invest in their own human capital to better prepare for jobs.

The trends are clear that the prolonged period to find jobs and careers is here to stay. But our twentieth-century education system is woefully out of sync with this twenty-first-century economy that demands highly knowledgeable and flexible workers.

In the future, higher education for most people will become less of a phase we enter at eighteen years old and exit at twenty-two. Instead, college will be a starting platform for lifelong learning that we step off and on when we need further education and training to get ahead in our jobs or switch careers. More of our education will be "just in time" rather than "just one time." And it will be delivered by a wider array of providers—the traditional colleges we have today but also emerging outfits that offer short- and long-form courses.

It's not good enough anymore to simply gain admission

to a top college and then roll into the job market. You have some time to figure this out, but to navigate the new pathways and various on- and off-ramps, you need a business plan for life that engages your talents and interests.

To help you write that plan, the heart of this book is a how-to, structured around the key markers for adolescents as they march toward adulthood: the pathway to college, the college experience itself, and, of course, the critical first years after graduation.

It lists the skills today's employers are seeking (and not getting) and describes how many more teenagers are taking a break from the often rushed transition from high school to college with gap experiences. It explores why the physical location of the college you attend matters more than ever in securing the hands-on experiences you need to get the right job after graduation. It examines the post-college launch and arms students with the job skills they need.

The final part of the book outlines the future of work, how companies will hire, and how tomorrow's college graduates can better translate their experiences and skills into a coherent story to succeed.

As I was starting the reporting for this book, I came across a study from Oxford University stating that nearly half of American jobs were at risk of being displaced in the future by automation and artificial intelligence. History has shown such predictions to be wildly exaggerated, of course. The story of the twentieth century is one of rising automation and better jobs with higher pay. The Harvard economists Claudia Goldin and Lawrence Katz have found that in the long race between education and technology, education has always won.

But this time things seem different. Young adults are doing everything their parents and guidance counselors tell them to do, and yet they are still failing to find secure jobs that lead to lifelong careers.

Plenty of twentysomethings are thriving, however, by drawing their own maps to navigate a turbulent, unpredictable world very different from the one my generation entered two decades ago. My hope is that this book will help to dispel your fears about life after college.

CHAPTER 1

THE SPRINTERS, WANDERERS, AND STRAGGLERS

STANLEY HALL GREW UP IN THE TINY VILLAGE OF ASHFIELD, MASSACHUSETTS, NEAR THE FOOTHILLS OF THE BERKSHIRE MOUNTAINS IN THE NORTHwest corner of the state. At age eighteen, he left home for Williams College, just thirty-five miles away, with a goal to "do something and be something in the world." His parents were farmers. His mother, Abigail, wanted her son to become a minister, but young Stanley wasn't sure about that plan. He had different ideas about college; he saw the four-year degree as a rite of passage—a chance to follow his passions and to explore.

Though Stanley excelled academically at Williams—he was voted smartest in his class—his parents considered his undergraduate years a bit erratic. When he graduated from college, he told his mom he didn't think he had the "requirements for a pastor." Even so, he moved to New York City and enrolled in a seminary.

The big city was intoxicating, and living there persuaded Stanley to abandon his religious studies short of a degree, and at the age of twenty-five, after securing a loan, he set off for Germany to study philosophy. While there, Stanley traveled extensively, visiting the theaters, bars, and dance halls of Berlin.

"What exactly are you doing over there?" his father sternly asked him.

He added physiology and physics to his academic pursuits and told his parents he was thinking about getting a Ph.D. in philosophy. His mother questioned the benefit of a Ph.D. "Just what is a Doctor of Philosophy?" she asked.

His parents wanted him to come home and get a real job, and even Stanley wondered what was next. He felt he was drifting through his twenties.

"I am twenty-five and have done nothing for myself, scarcely tried my hand in the world to know where I can do anything," he told his parents. But he continued his studies and explored Germany for a few more years. By then, Stanley was out of money, in debt, and without an advanced degree, so he returned home to the United States after his parents refused to support him financially. He was twenty-seven years old.

The Ever-Lengthening Road to Adulthood

STANLEY HALL'S STORY IS SIMILAR TO THAT OF MANY young Americans today. They go off to college, resist their parents' pressures to choose a job-connected major, and then drift through the years after college graduation, often short of money or any real plan. But here's the difference: Stanley Hall grew up in a totally different America—the one of the late 1800s.

We think this kind of lengthy takeoff is a relatively new situation for parents, but it's not. Sure, the timetable to adulthood is definitely longer now than ever before and affects far more people, but even at the turn of the twentieth century, when the economy offered fewer career choices for people like Hall and far fewer had college degrees, young people still roamed around throughout their twenties.

Hall eventually started a career—he earned an advanced degree, taught at Antioch College and Harvard University, married in his midthirties, and became president of Clark University in Massachusetts. While at Clark, he developed a fascination with the period in life between childhood and adulthood. He founded the American Psychological Association, and in the early 1900s, he wrote an influential book that coined a new life stage that he called "adolescence."

Hall described this transitional period from childhood to adulthood, between the ages of fourteen and twenty-four, as being full of "storm and stress." Industrialization and automation, along with child labor laws, meant that teenagers no longer had to work in the factories or on the farms. And the emergence of the high school movement in the United States required children to acquire more education before entering the workforce.

In reality, the adolescent stage in the early 1900s was much shorter than Hall described. Employers didn't demand that most teenagers go to college, so they were able to get a solid full-time job after graduating from high school, followed quickly by marriage and parenthood. Then around the middle of the last century, the job market began requiring that more young Americans add a college degree to the equation. The timetable to adulthood lengthened to the middle of a person's twenties, although it was still short by today's standards.

After World War II, the GI Bill allowed returning veterans, mostly men, to go to college for free, and the fast-growing postwar workforce quickly absorbed them. They got married, bought houses in the developing suburbs, and had kids, achieving all those key milestones in their twenties. Between 1950 and 1960, the percentage of men nineteen to twenty-four years old living with their parents fell by half.

That post–World War II era cemented in our minds an idea that remains to this day: teenagers graduate from high school, earn a college degree, secure a job, and move out of their childhood home—all by the age of twenty-two or so. But the 1950s turned out to be an anomaly in a century-long extension of the timetable to adulthood. World War II forced many adolescents, drafted to serve, to grow up before they were really ready to be adults; the GI Bill made it easy and cheap to go to college; and companies were quick to hire a new crop of college-educated veterans, as the United States faced little global competition from countries still rebuilding from the war.

Yet by the 1960s, the trend of a quick launch to adulthood was ending, and by the 1970s, young twentysomethings started living with their parents in larger numbers. In other words, the "boomerang generation," named for college graduates who return home to live with their parents today, existed forty years ago, too. It was just much smaller.

The difference between then and now is that manufacturing was still the foundation of the U.S. economy. In 1970, factory work accounted for 25 percent of jobs nationwide (compared with 10 percent today). Even in the bad economy of the 1970s, a college degree wasn't necessary for financial success, allowing more than one pathway to solid middle-class jobs for most young people. At that time, the wage premium for a college degree—how much more the typical bachelor's degree recipient earned compared with a high school graduate—was below 40 percent. In 1976, *Newsweek* ran a cover story asking "Who Needs College?" with a picture of two college graduates in their caps and gowns on a construction site with a jackhammer and a shovel, suggesting that as much as "27 percent of the nation's work force may now be made up of people who are 'overeducated' for the jobs they hold."

But the 1970s marked the last full decade when a large slice of the population didn't need a college degree. The recession of the early 1980s effectively killed off manufacturing in the United States, and the next decade's technology revolution essentially mandated education after high school. The economic benefits of World War II had finally ended. The increase in the wage premium started to speed up for college graduates, and after 1983, it turned into a runaway train. In 1983, the wage premium was 42 percent. Today, it surpasses 80 percent.

The high school movement of the early 1900s, which brought about the new life stage of adolescence, turned into the universal college movement as we neared the end of the twentieth century. College did not become that much more valuable, but the loss of many blue-collar jobs caused the high school diploma to become much less valuable. More education was necessary in a knowledge economy, and acquiring that education required a longer timetable between adolescence and adulthood. Beginning in 1980, the next three decades would see a massive run-up in the number of students enrolled in college (both undergraduate and graduate students), leading to further delays in passing the milestones of adulthood, from marriage to buying a house, and forever changing how we view what had been a predictable transition from education to the workforce.

The Three Pathways to a Career

TODAY, THOSE IN THEIR LATE TEENS AND EARLY TWENTIES don't seem to fit either the traditional definition of adolescent *or* young adult. They are living in more of an in-between period.

In the 1990s, Jeffrey Jensen Arnett, a psychology professor at the University of Missouri, interviewed young people around the country and determined that his interview subjects felt both grown-up and not-quite-so-grown-up at exactly the same time. This led Arnett to conclude that this period between ages eighteen and twenty-five was a distinct stage separate from both adolescence *and* young adulthood. In 2000, he published a paper conceiving a new term for this slice of life: "emerging adulthood."

"Emerging adults often explore a variety of possible life directions in love, work, and world views," Arnett wrote at the time. "Emerging adulthood is a time of life when many different directions remain possible, when little about the future has been decided for certain, when the scope of independent exploration of life's possibilities is greater for most people than it will be at any other period of the life course."

The phrase "emerging adults" immediately entered the cultural lexicon, especially for parents trying to figure out why their children were struggling to launch into adulthood. It was cited thousands of times by the media and other academics. Arnett wrote several books on the subject and became a sought-after speaker by educators and corporate executives trying to understand young people, millennials in particular.

By the time I caught up with Arnett in 2014, he had moved to Clark University, the same campus in Massachusetts where Stanley Hall had ended up as president in the early 1900s. Fourteen years after Arnett coined the term, I was curious to hear whether the journey to adulthood was getting even longer for the emerging adults of this decade. "Absolutely," he told me. Arnett said he had deliberately avoided using generational terms to describe what those in their late teens and early twenties were undergoing "because the changes that are happening are permanent structural changes that have only sped up all over the world."

This stuttering route to adulthood is now the new normal for most kids, transcending generations and occurring regardless of the economy's health. The stark reality hasn't totally discouraged this generation of emerging adults, however. Indeed, they have come to accept it as part of their lives. In his research, Arnett found emerging adults to be a largely optimistic bunch. Nearly 90 percent of those eighteen to twenty-nine years old told Clark University pollsters in 2012—in the midst of a global economic slowdown—they were confident they would eventually get what they wanted out of life. Another 83 percent said they believed "anything is possible." This optimism made them feel they could take their time in finding the right career niche without becoming cynical about the world or worrying about providing for a family.

When it came to the subject of education after high school, however, emerging adults and those who had recently moved into adulthood appeared much more unsettled. They definitely wanted to further their education but were not quite sure how to pay for it. Nearly six in ten people twenty-five to thirty-nine years old surveyed by Arnett in 2014—a group he called "established adults"—said they wished they had completed more years of education to move up in their careers. Another 70 percent in that poll expected to go back to school at some point, although some 40 percent were unable to get the credentials they needed because of a lack of money.

Arnett told me that for today's emerging adults, a college education—and not just going to college but actually earning a degree—is the biggest determinant of whether twentysomethings launch into a sustaining career or not. He's certainly not alone in believing that. In the last decade, scores of economists, sociologists, and psychologists alike have described the critical role a college degree plays in the divergent paths young adults eventually take.

That's still true. But it's not *just* the college degree that separates the successful from the drifters these days. If that were the case, recent college graduates wouldn't be standing in the unemployment line or settling for jobs that don't require a bachelor's degree. While some sort of degree after high school remains the foundation of a successful life and career, other coming-of-age, real-world experiences in the late teens and early twenties—particularly apprenticeships, jobs, or internships—actually matter more nowadays in moving from college to a career.

Today's emerging adults make that transition in one of three ways: they are either *Sprinters, Wanderers,* or *Stragglers* in the race to adulthood.

THE SPRINTERS:
Investments in Human Capital Pay Off

The Sprinters by their nature start fast right out of the gate from college. Some have the perfect job lined up, and others are laser-like in their focus, moving from job to job quickly up the career ladder. But speed alone doesn't define this group. Some are slow but methodical, assembling the building blocks for a successful career early on, mostly by going to graduate or professional school and investing more in their own human capital before hitting the job market. Others collect the right internships and postgraduate experiences, which add key markers to their résumés so they are ready to pounce when the right opportunity comes along.

While we imagine this is how most graduates should start out, only one-third of twentysomethings are Sprinters, according to a survey of 752 young adults ages twenty-four to twenty-seven conducted for this book (see full results in the appendix). They are not defined by one set of qualities, but many I met, and those in the survey, share several attributes. They had a job in high school (even at minimum wage) and understand the nuances and basic requirements of the workplace (such as showing up on time). They picked a major early on in college and stuck with it. This allowed them to dedicate time to outside-the-classroom pursuits, such as research projects or internships (79 percent had at least one internship in college, according to my own survey).

They also have little or no student loan debt, freeing them to pick job opportunities without regard to pay (my survey found 33 percent had less than $10,000 of debt). Whether they went to an elite or not-so-selective college, most came from families willing to support them—many with financial help, others with simple encouragement—as they landed on their feet in their early twenties.

Lily Cua is a classic Sprinter. Well before she got her degree in finance from Georgetown University, she secured a plum position as a consultant with PricewaterhouseCoopers. The job emerged like so many do these days, from a summer internship at the firm. She had applied for the internship her junior year as a way to practice her interviewing skills. The recruiter, a Georgetown alumnus, was impressed with her Chinese minor and high grades—signals, he told her, that she was willing to take on demanding assignments. "They really wanted someone who was interested in learning and working hard," she recalled. By the end of the summer she was offered a full-time job, ten months before graduation. "It wasn't my dream to work there," she admitted. But she took the job because she knew it would provide her with a launching pad.

She saw it not as a career in itself, but as a means to jumpstart her twenties. That's how many college seniors view such consulting positions. It's like getting paid to go to graduate school. And a gig with a big consulting firm can look as good on a résumé as a master's degree, with the added bonus of providing young graduates with a network of coworkers in various stages of their career.

"I wanted to learn," Lily told me. "I wanted to get skills I didn't have coming out of college. I wanted to work with really smart people. I wanted to be mentored by someone looking out for me."

I met Lily at 1776, an incubator in Washington, D.C., that assists start-up companies. It houses some 210 start-ups, and it's crawling with Sprinters like her. After two years with PricewaterhouseCoopers, she left to launch a business with a college acquaintance. Their company has already raised more than $400,000 for an online marketplace that allows employers to give their workers more choices in perks and benefits. She says the process of deciding to leave a Fortune 500 firm so early in her life was "all consuming," but she, like most Sprinters, recognized that the early twenties are the best time to take risks and try new things. Few of them have a mortgage, spouse, or kids, so the price of failure is typically pretty low and the potential reward is exponentially higher. If their choices don't work out, it's easy for them to quickly start all over again.

That makes Sprinters unafraid to change jobs frequently in their twenties. The average American holds eight different jobs between the ages of eighteen and twenty-nine. For the average college graduate, it takes four years to find a job that will last five years or more. Such job hopping is typically seen as a lack of commitment or direction—and it could be—but not if it's done to advance in a career or to try out different occupations.

Switching jobs in your twenties actually boosts your chances for more satisfying and higher-paying work in the decades that follow. Henry Siu calls it "job shopping" for a better match. Siu, an associate professor at the Vancouver School of Economics at the University of British Columbia, was part of a team of economists that examined more than thirty years of unemployment data in the United States. In a study the group published in 2014, the economists found that increased mobility in a person's twenties leads to higher earnings later on in life, when people are less able to move or can't easily abandon the skills they have learned.

College should prepare graduates to be "occupationally footloose," Siu told me, meaning they can perform a variety of entry-level jobs in different occupations while they are young. Twentysomethings have always changed jobs. The difference now, according to Siu, is that one in three of them changes *occupations* on a regular basis, a much higher proportion than in previous generations.

According to Siu, "we are living in an increasingly complex society with many more choices for occupations," more than anyone can reasonably explore while in college. So trying out different occupations is now a part of life for twentysomethings, another reason they need a longer runway to adulthood.

Unfortunately, a growing number of emerging adults lack

the financial flexibility to change jobs or to take low-paying positions that might be great career starters. Their problem? Student loans.

Of those who financed college through loans, the average class of 2014 graduate left commencement day $33,000 in debt. Six months later, those graduates received their first payment notice in the mail, on average for about $380, with 120 more monthly payments ahead of them. That figure might not seem like much, but when it accounts for about 15 percent of an average new graduate's take-home salary, it can have an impact on the career decisions someone makes when just starting out. Salary—not fit, happiness, or career advancement—becomes the driving decision in choosing a job. Debt rules out unpaid internships that could lead to a top-notch job, for example, or living in pricey cities with dynamic labor markets that offer twentysomethings many job options.

A friend who works at a major magazine publisher in New York City described salaries for entry-level jobs there that barely break $40,000 in one of the most expensive cities in the world. Most people in those jobs, she said, depend on their parents to subsidize their living expenses. This arrangement is not that uncommon. About half of those who graduated from college in 2011, and were tracked by an extensive University of Arizona study, reported relying on financial support from parents, including those who were employed full-time. About six in ten college students need to take on some debt to pay for school. When searching for colleges, be sure to compare the average debt at graduation; a large loan can greatly influence job decisions for the rest of your life.

This impact of student debt on career choices is a relatively recent occurrence. In 1989, only 17 percent of twentysome-things had student debt; today, 42 percent do. The polling firm Gallup, which measures well-being on five metrics, including financial, physical, and having a purpose in life, has found that "the more student loan debt you have, the less likely you are to be thriving in your well-being," said Brandon Busteed, who heads up its education division.

Busteed wasn't surprised when I told him that nearly every young person I met at 1776 had no student loan debt. According to Gallup's polling data, most entrepreneurs owe less than $10,000 in student loans. Having debt greater than that figure has a negative impact on the decision to start a business. Considering that start-ups create jobs at a faster clip than legacy companies, if we have fewer emerging adults willing to take a chance on their business ideas because they must pay down student loans, it will only be harder for everyone else with a college degree to get a job.

THE WANDERERS:
Stuttered Steps to a Career

Valerie Lapointe is one of those college graduates trying to find work. When I met her for coffee in Washington, D.C., a few weeks before Christmas, she was studying for the GRE. Her job search had stalled, and she had decided to do what many recent college graduates do when they get stuck: go back to school for yet another degree.

The master's degree is quickly becoming the new bachelor's degree. In 2013, about 760,000 master's degrees were awarded, a number that has increased 250 percent since 1980 and is rising at a much faster pace than those earning a bachelor's degree. Nearly 30 percent of recent graduates are back in school within two years of getting a bachelor's degree (although enrollment is beginning to flatten, as we'll see in Chapter 8). For them, graduate school is akin to having a job because it gives them structure and direction.

As we sipped our coffee, Valerie quipped about the relevance of our setting. After all, coffee shops have become emblematic of those wandering through their twenties. The Starbucks barista with a bachelor's degree is the stereotype for the underemployed. And these days coffee shops are a popular place for young adults to hang out as they search for jobs or work on freelance projects.

"I have applied for jobs from here to kingdom come," she said. "When you are unemployed, you can apply for jobs all day." She likened her job search to dating. "You look great on paper, they interview you, but then they never call you back. You get used to the rejection."

Valerie is twenty-five years old, with shoulder-length blond hair and a smile as quick as her wit. She grew up in the nearby affluent suburbs of northern Virginia. She graduated from a top-notch high school with a 3.9 grade point average in the spring of 2008, a year marked by a boom in the number of eighteen-year-olds across the country (so lots of competition to get into the college of her choice) as well as one of the worst economic crashes in the nation's history (meaning lots of unemployed recent college graduates).

"I had no idea what I wanted to do with my life when I went to college," she told me.

I asked her why she didn't delay going to college, take

time off to explore her interests before she committed to a school.

"There was never a question in my parents' mind that I'd go directly on to college, the question was just where," she said. "It had worked out for them, so why not me?"

I heard similar stories from many recent graduates who had college-educated parents: the expectation that college, especially a four-year school, was the *only* pathway right out of high school, no detours allowed, such as a gap year to discover their interests or exploring majors by taking courses at a local community college.

Valerie took the direct route. Wait-listed at James Madison University, she instead landed at the University of Mary Washington, a public college in south-central Virginia, not far from the state capital of Richmond. Still unsure about a major, Valerie's schedule was mostly filled with general education courses her first two years. Then she took a journalism class with a former reporter for the *Wall Street Journal,* and she was hooked.

But Mary Washington didn't have a journalism major. So Valerie found as many writing courses as she could and joined the student newspaper. She thought about transferring to a school with a journalism major, but she was on track to finish her bachelor's degree in just three years and save money. "By the time I figured it out, it was too late," she said.

It was too late for her to join the Sprinters.

Valerie instead fell back in the pack among those with college degrees. She became a Wanderer, part of a growing number of young adults I met who are drifting through their midtwenties and largely treading water in the years after college graduation.

It's not for a lack of motivation or hard work. They are certainly not—as the headlines often make them out to be—either lazy or entitled. At eighteen, they were unsure what they wanted to do in life. So they were relegated to the assembly line by parents and guidance counselors and expected to build their adult selves there. Their first pass was through college, where the assembly line is moving faster than ever before: pick a major, secure internships, take classes in the right order to graduate on time. Most students, though, can't keep up that pace.

A quarter of all freshmen change their major by the end of their first year, and half of first-year students say they plan to switch their field of study. Switching majors, in and of itself, doesn't mean you'll definitely land among the Wanderers, especially if you end up with greater clarity about what you want to do as a result. But only about half of students finish a bachelor's degree in four years, let alone have the internships, the leadership positions in campus activities, or research projects sought by the top employers these days. So Wanderers start behind before they even get into the job market. About half of the 1.7 million seniors of the class of 2014 were unable to land a full-time job within six months of graduation.

Valerie did take a job as a nanny and saved money by living at home. By the time she started seriously looking for a job in her field a year and a half after graduation, she was already competing with the next crop of college graduates. She paid to enroll in a summer internship program that got her a job in public relations at a think tank, which she took in the hopes that it would lead to better employment prospects. It didn't. She took a road trip to Los Angeles with a friend, before returning to Washington to work as a hostess. She landed a job at a video production company but got laid off after three months. Since then she has patched together a series of jobs as a nanny and through temp agencies.

"I knew it would be difficult, but not this difficult," she told me. Signing on to Facebook sometimes makes her feel even further behind, as friends post the highlights of their daily lives. "I honestly believed that by twenty-five I'd have more of my life together."

There are millions of college graduates like Valerie throughout the country—they earned a college degree but run into trouble along the way to adulthood. Many are derailed right out of college. They settle for any paying job because of financial pressures, or they move back home because of family obligations. Some don't know how to get started in a career and bypass meaningful internships or jobs because they find them menial or they can't afford to live on a paltry salary (or in the cases of some internships, none at all). And some, like Valerie, go back to school and usually go deeper into debt. In one study, total student debt tripled for those not working while in graduate school, from $22,000 to $76,000. The bright future that seemed possible for so many of them on the first day of college spirals quickly out of reach, all in the course of just a few years.

But all is not lost for the Wanderer. My own survey of twentysomethings found that 32 percent of young adults are Wanderers, although some are wandering more than others.

As a whole, they are more likely to go to public colleges, where they are less than certain of their major when they enter. Eighty-five percent of them after graduation begin working in a job unrelated to their major.

Some Wanderers actually have a plan. The Starbucks barista might be saving for graduate school or taking care of an ailing parent in the short term. "It's important to have clarity about where you want to go, knowing you can change the way of getting there," said Andy Chan, who heads up career services at Wake Forest University.

Just how circuitous a path Wanderers take in getting where they want to go in life is what they should worry most about. The twenties have been called a "dress rehearsal" for the rest of life. Lingering instability during this period eventually leads to problems down the road. Perhaps most critical is that the bulk of a worker's salary increases tend to come in the first decade of employment. For men, in particular, three-quarters of their wage growth happens in just these first ten years.

Graduating in an economic downturn, like the United States has experienced since 2008, puts even more pressure on those in their twenties. Lisa Kahn, an economist at Yale University, found that when students graduate from college in a weak economy, they have lower earnings even fourteen to twenty-three years later on in life. The graduating classes immediately following the 2008 recession, for instance, even now earn a third less than those who left college just a few years earlier and had a better economic footing getting started. New graduates don't shop for jobs as much in a bad economy, Kahn said, and job shopping is how they get bigger paychecks in those critical first years after college.

Lagging salaries affect all aspects of life for college graduates, from their ability to purchase a home to the tendency to acquire excessive credit card debt. "Graduates' first jobs have an inordinate impact on their career path and 'future income stream,'" observes Austan Goolsbee, former chairman of the Council of Economic Advisers under President Obama and an economics professor at the University of Chicago. "People essentially cannot close the wage gap by working their way up the company hierarchy. While they may work their way up, the people who started above them do, too." The longer Wanderers drift through their twenties, the longer the runway becomes for them and the harder it becomes to catch up. And those who don't ever quite find the on-ramp in their midtwenties eventually end up joining the last group to get in the career line: the Stragglers.

THE STRAGGLERS:
Drifting Through Their Twenties

On a crisp, early fall evening in September, I found myself in Portland, Oregon, with a few hours to spare before a red-eye flight back to Washington, D.C. The previous Sunday, the *New York Times Magazine* published a story about how the city was becoming a place where "young people go to retire," to steal the tag line from the satirical television show *Portlandia,* which is set there.

Even though they were not finding good-paying jobs, the article said twentysomethings were remaining nonetheless, attracted by the city's nearby mountains, mild winters, outdoorsy reputation, and streak of independence. In some ways, Portland had become a magnet for Stragglers—those who spend much of their twenties looking for what they were meant to do. I had come here to find out why it took Stragglers so long.

In Portland's eastside industrial district, I met up with Josh Mabry. Tall, with a military buzz cut and forearms filled with tattoos, Josh was about to turn thirty. He was a prototypical Straggler. After a decade of dead-end jobs and false starts at a handful of colleges, Josh told me he was finally settling into something he cared about: woodworking. Josh always liked working with his hands. His father and grandfather were woodworkers. But he took his last woodshop class in seventh grade. By high school, he said, guidance counselors were pushing the idea of going to college.

"I thought about studying psychology, but I was bored of school," he said, a common refrain I heard from many Stragglers. Instead, he went to work on a residential construction crew the summer after high school. "I really enjoyed it, finishing a project and seeing it come together," he said. At the end of the summer, Josh followed a girlfriend two hours south to Eugene. Unable to find a construction job, he enrolled in graphic design classes at Lane Community College. He fell into the party scene there, and after a few years he returned to Portland and took a job as a bartender to pay the bills.

"I was drifting," he told me.

That defined much of the next decade for him. He tried two other community colleges in the area, dabbling in welding and forestry. "I wanted the skill set, not the piece of paper," Josh said. He dropped out of school twice. He took off to Central America for eight months, taking on bartending gigs in between. Then at twenty-nine years old, he saw a flyer for a local facility in Portland that was offering short-term woodworking, metalworking, and upholstery classes. He signed up for a metalworking class and followed that with a few woodworking classes. Josh had finally found his passion. He began to make wooden light fixtures and art pieces. He set up a website and now sells his products online.

"I knew that by the time I turned thirty I needed to figure something out for myself," he said. "I finally have some sort of path."

The pathway to a career takes Stragglers much longer to carve out because many of them struggle to find viable options after high school to mature and explore careers beyond just going to college. And if they go to college, most of them struggle to finish, and many don't at all. My survey found that about one-third of those in their midtwenties are Stragglers. Nearly 40 percent of them took time off after high school for nonacademic reasons (not a gap year, as we'll explore in Chapter 3). A little more than half of the slowest of the Stragglers failed to find work immediately after college. It didn't help that only one in four of them pursued an internship while in school.

While today's economy demands more than a high school diploma, if you're an eighteen-year-old not motivated to go to college or not quite ready intellectually or financially, the alternatives available to you are pretty limited. You can stay at home, get a job (and not a very good one), or join the military (a declining option for many). No wonder 95 percent of high school seniors say they plan to attend college, and nearly 70 percent of them do so the fall after they graduate.

They often go because there is simply nothing else for them to do. College is a warehouse until they're ready for adulthood.

Of course, teachers and guidance counselors who push college right after high school rarely know what happens to most of their graduates. They probably don't want to know. The news is not good. Many students end up dropping out of college, usually in the first few semesters. There are some 12.5 million twentysomethings with *some* college credits and *no* degree. Indeed, those in their twenties make up by far the largest share of the 31 million adults in the United States who left college short of a degree. In many ways, these young adults are no better off financially than high school graduates who never attempted college at all. Employers, after all, don't advertise that they want "some college." They want a degree.

The collapse of American manufacturing in the 1980s left the United States with a one-size-fits-all route through college that educators continue to press on students and their families from a very young age. The college-for-all movement is not a cure-all for the Americans who never end up finishing their degree. But it's almost impossible in our hypercompetitive culture to think differently as a parent about *when* a college education should happen for your kids.

The longer life expectancy for children born today means that we can chart new routes to adulthood that space out opportunities in different ways from how we planned in the last century. We no longer should think of college as *one physical place* we go to at *one time* in our lives at the age of eighteen. Yet for too many American teenagers that's exactly how they are programmed. The result: finding a pathway to a fulfilling career and a meaningful life has become much more difficult than it ever should have been.

What Will Become of the "Vast Middle"?

THE RECOMMENDED ROUTE THROUGH COLLEGE TO A career has sparked an unprecedented surge in enrollment on campuses over the last two decades. The number of undergraduates nationwide has grown by 8 million students since 1980, according to the National Center for Education Statistics.

But those students weren't spread out evenly across thousands of colleges and universities nationwide. The most elite colleges—household brand names like Harvard, Stanford, or Amherst—are essentially the same size today as they were several decades ago. The increased demand for a spot on campus has just made it harder—some would say impossible—for nearly all the students who apply to get into them. Even the best public universities, places such as the University of Michigan at Ann Arbor, the University of North Carolina at Chapel Hill, the University of Virginia, or the University of California at Berkeley, haven't expanded their student populations to keep up with demand. Rather, the increase in high school graduates going off to college has occurred at second-tier public universities and community colleges already stretched thin.

Oregon State University is an example of a university that has been expected to do more with less money from state coffers. The university's enrollment has nearly doubled in size since 2000. Before I met Josh Mabry in Portland, I was in rural Corvallis, where I spent the day on Oregon State's campus. There Professor Rick Settersten was teaching his class on critical thinking to several dozen students, mostly seniors.

The classroom conversation wandered to a discussion about their own futures, what they wanted to do next in life. Many said they planned to go on to graduate school. Settersten asked how many of them knew their professors well enough to request a letter of recommendation. Only a smattering of hands went up. Settersten wondered aloud why more of them didn't visit him during office hours, an easy way to build a one-on-one relationship with a professor who teaches sometimes hundreds of students in a semester. "What shocked me is that they say, 'No one has told me this before,'" Settersten said to me later. "They're seniors and they don't know how to navigate the institution."

Settersten has a boyish face framed by brown-rimmed glasses. His academic research focuses on what it means to become an adult in America today. Unlike many parents and media pundits, he doesn't worry as much about the longer runway to adulthood, arguing that the timetable to becoming an adult is more gradual and varied today than it was fifty years ago. The traditional markers such as marriage and parenting are now the *culmination* of becoming an adult rather than the *start* of it.

"The postponement of these transitions has freed up the early adult years such that young people today actually live *more* independently, not less," Settersten wrote in the *Washington Post* in 2014. I asked him about the somewhat clueless students in his class; doesn't he worry about them? "Sure," he said. "When I think of adult life, one of the hallmarks of it is that it's not predictable."

The problem is that colleges have attempted to make the four-year experience *more* predictable in recent years by adding a bevy of advising services and amenities for students so that essentially everything is done for them to ensure they graduate on time and secure a job afterward. Though these programs may indeed help students graduate, they prevent them from building the resilience they will need as adults to manage risk and succeed in unpredictable careers or lives.

In college, "there are things you're taught and then there are things you learn," Settersten told me. "A lot of what college comes down to is not what happens in the classroom. It's about navigating life and building relationships." But only about half of college seniors on campuses nationwide say they talk often with a faculty member about their career plans, according to the National Survey of Student Engagement, an annual poll of freshmen and seniors.

Graduates who start slow and linger through their early career are often those who didn't take college seriously while on campus. They avoid rigorous majors and courses and focus more on the social scene than academics. In 2011, two sociologists, Richard Arum and Josipa Roksa, published a book called *Academically Adrift: Limited Learning on College Campuses* that described just how much students actually learned in college. The results were devastating—at least to students and parents who had mortgaged their life to pay for school. The pair found that 45 percent of the 1,600 students they tracked at a diverse set of twenty-five colleges and universities made no gains in their writing, complex reasoning, or critical thinking skills during their first two years of college. After four years, the news wasn't much better: 36 percent failed to show any improvement.

Of those students who didn't learn much in college, what happened after they graduated? Arum and Roksa wanted to find out and tracked down nearly a thousand of them two years after commencement for a follow-up book, *Aspiring Adults Adrift,* which they published in 2014. What they found was as distressing as what they said in their first book, but not much of a surprise. Poor academic performers in college were more likely than other recent graduates to be unemployed, stuck in unskilled jobs, or to have been fired or laid off from their jobs after graduation. Where students went to college didn't matter two years out, the two authors found, as much as what they did while they were on campus.

"The most important choice students can make is whether they are on the party-social pathway through college," Arum told me, "or are investing sufficient attention and focus on academic pursuits."

Too many students, even some who end up becoming Sprinters, see college as a four-year vacation. College students in 1961 dedicated twenty-four hours a week to studying outside the classroom. By 2003, that fell to fourteen hours.

Like Jeffrey Jensen Arnett before them, Arum and Roksa found hope and optimism among recent college graduates despite their life circumstances. Two-thirds of them said their lives would be better than those of their parents, although they really had no idea how that would happen. For some students, mostly the Sprinters, carving that path to a better life was not going to be a problem.

"There are exceptional students," Arum said. "There are just not enough of them." He is concerned about the vast middle, the Wanderers. "The system is not working for large numbers of students and I very much worry about their ability to be successful in the long run."

The longer timetable to adulthood is here to stay. How those in their late teens and early twenties use that time to acquire the skills and attributes the economy needs and employers demand will determine whether they become Sprinters, Wanderers, or Stragglers in the first decade of their career.

CHAPTER 2

WHAT THE ECONOMY NEEDS, WHAT EMPLOYERS WANT

BM'S ALMADEN RESEARCH CENTER SITS AT THE TOP OF SEVEN HUNDRED ACRES OF SERENE, UNDEVELOPED LAND OVERLOOKING THE SPRAWL OF SILICON VALLEY. The 540,000-square-foot facility opened in 1986, at the dawn of the personal computer age when IBM was a technology behemoth, years before there was any inkling of Google and Facebook, and decades before we began to imagine the technology for the iPhone and streaming music services.

It employs several hundred top-notch Ph.D. researchers and scientists who have been responsible for discoveries that most of us will never fully understand but have undoubtedly made our lives better: the first Internet connection in 1988, the first data-mining algorithms in 1994, and the world's smallest disk drive in 1998.

The lab is reached by taking a winding, narrow two-lane

road off a busy highway until you reach a small entry gate at the top. Only a small sign with the iconic IBM logo indicates that you have arrived at Almaden, a low-rise, modern green building with breathtaking panoramic views of the surrounding valley.

I visited Almaden on a late March day to meet with Jim Spohrer, a computer scientist who leads IBM's university partnerships. Part of Spohrer's job is to ensure that colleges are teaching the skills needed for employment at IBM and to attract talented students to work at the company. IBM hires thousands of college graduates each year, so what the company looks for in potential employees matters far beyond these walls.

As we walked toward his office, Spohrer told me that when the Almaden Research Center opened, IBM recruited candidates who were mostly expert in one subject. They could write computer code, for instance, and do it really well. IBM then trained new employees in the "IBM way." Though IBM still spends $600 million a year on training, the company and the world around it are much more complex than they were even in the 1980s. IBM's training is not enough.

"IBM is in all industries—we do nanotechnology, quantum computing, systems research, modeling of industries, modeling of cities," Spohrer explained. Those adept in only one subject don't cut it in this modern work environment. Spohrer called them "I-shaped people." Today, employers need a different kind of talent: they want T-shaped individuals.

The idea of the T-shaped individual first emerged in the early 1990s as a kind of Renaissance man. The vertical bar of the T represents a person's deep understanding of one

subject matter—history, for example—as well as one industry, perhaps energy or health care. The horizontal stroke of
T-shaped people is the ability to work across a variety of
complex subject areas with ease and confidence. The need
for this ability is far greater today than it was two decades
ago as the world becomes more complicated technologically.

"You can only go so far as I-shaped in IBM—it's career
limiting," Spohrer said. "The people we like to work with
are T-shaped." Take a task such as detecting credit card fraud.
It requires skills in math, law, finance, technology, psychology, and political science. "We want people who can wrap
their head around the whole thing and be part of teams,"
Spohrer added.

I asked Spohrer how often he found T-shaped college
graduates who had both depth in a specific field and breadth
across academic disciplines. He shook his head. "Truth be
told, we would rather hire people from a start-up, acquire a
start-up, or hire them from a failed start-up than hire people
out of a university," he said. He explained that people with
start-up experience have the know-how to work in small
teams, find customers, and solve their problems. They have
initiative and persistence—what some call "grit"—to keep
going in the face of adversity. And they recognize the need
to spring back from failure quickly and learn from what
went wrong.

"In school, it's all about individual performance," Spohrer
said. "You better get it right the first time, because we're
going to test you. If you work in teams and something goes
wrong, you blame another team member. I'm less interested
in the big successes. People don't learn a lot from their successes, and they usually learn the wrong things."

There's more to being T-shaped than just having breadth and depth, however. It's also about having balance and the agility to pick and choose from a set of knowledge and skills as they are needed.

Undergraduates need to cultivate T-shaped skills to prepare for the economy they'll face after graduation. But too many students depend on their undergraduate years to spoon-feed them the experiences that will shape them for the future. They sit back and wait for professors to deliver lessons in the classroom. They participate in campus life but too often from the sidelines, so they lack any deep engagement in activities that provide much-needed skills for the job market. They fail to cultivate relationships with professors or staff on campus who might lend advice and act as mentors. And they are reluctant to chase after experiences—whether undergraduate research, study abroad, or internships—that help them discover their passions and arm them with the interpersonal skills so in demand by employers today.

You really can't blame them. Up to this point in their educational lives, school has been managed for them and, in the era of No Child Left Behind, increasingly so, as elementary and secondary schools hew closely to curriculum guides and teachers are focused on preparing students to take standardized tests. The advent of "my child can do no wrong" helicopter parents has exacerbated the problem, forcing a lowering of standards and, therefore, performance.

Here's the problem: colleges don't offer classes, majors, or activities designed specifically for building the T-shaped individual. So undergraduates need to direct themselves—to act independently, be resourceful, and cobble together experiences inside and outside the classroom to better prepare for the evolving workplace they will face in the future. They need to recognize that in high school their learning was directed for them by parents, teachers, and counselors, and they need to change into students who explore and discover what's next for them. Students need to self-direct their own learning, not just during their undergraduate years but for the rest of their lives as well.

The Skills Needed to Hit the Ground
Running After College

TO FIND OUT WHAT EXPERIENCES AND SKILLS EMPLOYERS want, I went to Burning Glass Technologies, a Boston-based company that analyzes job data in real time. Burning Glass was founded in 1999 at the dawn of the Big Data era, when superfast computers began allowing scientists to quickly comb massive amounts of digital information to discover detailed insights about people and their habits. Burning Glass focused on the key words hidden in job advertisements. It started mining the text of tens of millions of online postings to tease out the specific skills sought by employers.

The company's CEO is Matthew Sigelman, a slender, boyish-looking fortysomething Harvard Business School graduate and self-described data geek. Job advertisements obviously do not describe every skill an employer wants. Rather, he said, they are a screening device for the crucial skills a company needs and are probably not getting enough of in many candidates. Advertisements for lawyers don't say the candidates must have a law degree and have passed the bar exam, for instance. Anyone applying for an attorney's job must have those attributes as a baseline. Yet a careful reader will notice that job postings provide the best insight into the employer's needs and the skills most in demand in today's workplaces. A student interested in a job in a specific field or at a particular company should start reading these job listings for clues about what they are looking for.

Burning Glass analyzed the requirements listed in 20 million job postings across all industries in 2014 and compiled its list of the most requested "baseline skills." Sigelman described these as the broad competencies candidates need just to get in an employer's door. This analysis found that the number of baseline skills was actually fairly limited: twenty-five skills appeared in three out of every four job advertisements, no matter the industry.

Virtually every job posting included in its top five communication, writing, and organizational skills. Writing, for example, was an important skill even in information technology and health care jobs. Other competencies frequently requested across industries were a combination of soft skills—customer service, problem solving, planning, and being detail-oriented—as well as very specific hard skills—Microsoft Excel and Word. Bottom line: even if you're an English major, learn how to manipulate a spreadsheet by taking an online class or asking a friend.

Sigelman noted that soft skills—a term associated with how people get along with one another, communicate, and work in teams—appeared far more often than any technical skills. "It reflects a perception that students are coming to the market less job ready with these skills," Sigelman said.

That employers need to list soft skills at all indicates an underlying anxiety many recruiters expressed: the bachelor's degree may be the strongest signal that someone is ready for the job market, but it's become increasingly less reliable than it once was, in part because it doesn't indicate that students know the soft skills. The degree mostly indicates that they had the discipline to finish a task.

The Burning Glass analysis is compelling, but it showcases just one side of the hiring equation. It doesn't tell us anything about the people who were eventually hired for any of the jobs it analyzed. Having the skills listed in a job posting is important in one respect: it gets your résumé past automated software programs that many employers increasingly use to scan applications digitally. If you don't have those key words somewhere on your résumé, in your cover letter, or in an answer to a question on an application that the computer is looking for, it will likely delete your application.

But robots don't hire people. Eventually the final pool of applicants is interviewed by real people, a process full of gut decisions and hidden biases. Companies might say in a job advertisement they want applicants with certain skills but then hire someone for the job who doesn't possess them. Outcomes can't always be explained, but simply following the job ad as a formula to get in the door is like using a course syllabus as a guide to earn an A in the class.

Even within companies, wide inconsistencies exist between what the employer says it wants in its public marketing messages versus how it actually hires. One problem is that different people along the hiring chain in a company have varying goals for what they want from new college grads. Oftentimes, the CEO and the head of human resources— who have little or no contact with undergraduate hiring yet answer surveys on the subject—are searching for foundational qualities that will help new hires grow and stay for a career. Meanwhile, the direct supervisor for the position often wants to hire someone with the skills to fill the job today.

A few years ago at a conference, I heard A. G. Lafley, the recently retired CEO of Procter & Gamble, describe the merits of a liberal arts college degree (he himself is a graduate of a fine liberal arts school, Hamilton College, and he once wanted to become a professor in medieval and Renaissance history). Then while researching this book, I met a recruiter for Procter & Gamble who reminded me that, while Lafley might have an affinity for liberal arts colleges, as the top executive he doesn't actually hire any new college graduates. The recruiter told me that although Procter & Gamble is one of a few remaining employers that continues to invest in employee training, "we still expect our new hires to hit the ground running, and small liberal arts schools tend to prepare people for grad school." The recruiter I met favored students who graduated from engineering and business schools at large public universities and cited Purdue and Indiana Universities as two high on the list.

Corporate recruiters are the gatekeepers in hiring today's graduates. As I watched them pitch their companies in campus presentations and witnessed interviews with nervous undergraduates, I had the same question: Just what sort of education do students need in order to get a job after they graduate from college? I realized there was no clear answer. Articles about the jobs of the future might be popular clickbait on the web, but no one can accurately predict what careers in any field will look like in five, ten, or twenty years.

As I interviewed recruiters for large and small companies, from trendy employers like Facebook and eBay to the stalwarts on the campus job-fair circuit, such as Vanguard investments and Enterprise Rent-A-Car, a few themes emerged that went beyond just a specific list of skills or a diploma from a fancy university. Employers are increasingly looking past the degree and the transcript for a set of skills they believe are better markers of success for their new hires. If you are a college graduate hoping to get off to the right start, you will need to show you have acquired this set of often overlapping skills: *curiosity, creativity, grit, digital awareness, contextual thinking,* and *humility.*

1. Be Curious, Ask Questions, and Be a Learner for Life

Like most young children, my six- and four-year-old girls never stop asking questions. Why are there no stoplights on the highway? What is the capital on the other side of the world (we live in Washington, D.C.)? Why does it always storm in the summer? On average, preschool children ask their parents around one hundred questions a day. Why this, why that? I hear questions in my sleep. But eventually they ask fewer questions, and by the time they go to middle school they barely ask anything. That's unfortunate.

Educators and child psychologists have long wondered why kids lose their appetite for asking questions, and often they come to the same conclusion: school. In school, students are rewarded for having answers, not asking questions. By the time middle school rolls around, the peer effect takes over. Many kids worry about being embarrassed in front of their classmates for asking dumb questions or having the wrong answer. Young children don't have those worries yet. And they have plenty of free time in the early grades to exercise their curiosity (at least until the current infatuation with testing kicks in).

The fall my oldest daughter started prekindergarten, her school had just completed a major construction project. It had dozens of packing boxes left over from the move into the new space. Instead of taking the boxes directly to the recycling bin, it put them in a room, and my daughter's class was let loose to play with them. The children built a fort. They made a town. They constructed a school. It was the highlight of the week, perhaps the month, for her. She couldn't stop talking about the possibilities of what could be assembled with a bunch of cardboard boxes.

I wondered what would happen if a class of college seniors were put in that same room with the boxes. They'd ask plenty of questions, of course, but more about the process than the possibilities of what could be made: What's the assignment? Do we need to work in teams? How do we pick teams? When do we need to finish? How will we be graded?

Until students graduate from college, much of what they learn is necessarily guided by the teacher's syllabus or graduation requirements. But after college and for the rest of our lives, learning is self-directed. We decide what skills or knowledge we're missing, where to acquire that information, and how to fit learning into our daily routines. Unfortunately, by the time students graduate from college their brains are hardwired to the cadence of the daily life laid out by the nine-month academic calendar. They tend to think about their work in terms of fifty-minute classes and five courses over fifteen-week semesters, with plenty of lengthy breaks in between. College students spend only about a quarter of their week on academic pursuits—going to class or studying, or working at a job—leaving about half of their week for socializing and recreation, according to one survey.

No wonder colleges have spent hundreds of millions of dollars building palatial campus recreation centers with climbing walls in the last decade: students use them as often as they use classrooms. Friday has become the "collegiate day of rest," with many campuses offering far fewer classes on Fridays than other days, effectively training students for four-day workweeks.

But the working world is unstructured, with competing priorities and decisions that need to be made on the fly. "People know how to take a course, but they need to learn how to learn," John Leutner, head of global learning at Xerox, told me. At Xerox, young employees frequently request professional development courses on time management because in college someone else set their priorities for them. College is very task based: take an exam, finish a paper, attend a club meeting, go to practice. Meanwhile, the workplace is more of a mash-up of activities with no scheduled end.

The recent graduates who succeed in their careers are flexible about how they learn. "They have ideas and act on them," said Tim Brown, CEO of IDEO. "Being able to get stuff done is a capacity that is rather important."

You probably have never heard of IDEO. It's not a household brand name, yet it ranks among Apple, Google, and Facebook as one of Silicon Valley's hottest employers. Each year, some 20,000 people apply for about 150 job openings at the firm. Given those slim odds, I asked Brown what he looks for when hiring new employees. "Pie-shaped individuals," he said. Think of it as a twist on the T-shape, with the additional dimension of creativity.

IDEO is a consulting company fueled by creativity. While its roots are in industrial design—it was responsible for the first Apple computer mouse—these days it's perhaps as well known for designing customer experiences. Companies ranging from Holiday Inn to Kaiser Permanente turn to IDEO to solve a problem in the hopes of creating a breakthrough product or service. For example, it created the concept behind Bank of America's Keep the Change program, which encourages customers to save by rounding up the purchases on their debit cards to the nearest dollar and transferring the difference to their savings account.

What sets IDEO apart from most consulting firms is the range of expertise it brings to each task. Its teams include anthropologists, graphic designers, engineers, and psychologists. I asked Brown if an applicant's college major matters when hiring. Not unless it's an unusual combination, he said, like history and architecture. Most of all he's looking for a mind-set with creativity, passion, and empathy at its root. "I want a diversity of experiences in college that have exercised their brain," Brown said.

Just down the California coast from Silicon Valley is another critical sector of the economy that thrives on creativity, but today rarely finds among its ranks college graduates: the entertainment industry. A few years ago, I was invited to a meeting of entertainment executives from Netflix, Disney, ABC, Warner Bros., and a few others at the Soho House, a posh private club in West Hollywood.

The meeting was organized by the Entertainment Industry Foundation, the charitable arm of the movie and television industry that had produced the famous Stand Up to Cancer campaign. The foundation wanted to build a similar campaign for education. The members were worried about the state of the American system: too few students were pursuing rigorous courses in high school and too many were dropping out of college. Most of all, schools were turning out students trained to take tests, but who had no ability to come up with answers to problems not yet imagined. "Our industry is changing so fast that we can't depend on what students already know," one executive told the group. "We need people who are creative, curious, whose brains are wired to constantly ask what's next. What we need are learning animals."

In recent years, the entertainment industry has been one of the most resilient sectors during a period of lackluster economic growth. While the 2008 world financial crisis suffocated most economic activity, that year's production of movies, books, and video games all increased, some fourfold.

But even as Hollywood depends more on machine technology to produce and deliver movies, curiosity ultimately drives the growth in building creative products, said Bob Iger, Walt Disney's CEO. "If you don't seek to learn, you don't try new things," Iger told the movie producer Brian Grazer during a freewheeling conversation at the Milken Global Conference in Los Angeles. "I don't think you can run a business today in a very dynamic marketplace without being curious." When Iger interviews people for jobs, he asks them about the books they have read, the movies they have seen, or where they have recently traveled. "I try to get under their skin," he said, "to determine their level of curiosity."

Don't be mistaken, however. Creative industries in California are not the only places that want curious minds. Adam Bryant writes the Corner Office column in the Sunday edition of the *New York Times,* where he features interviews with executives about leadership and management. The topic of learning agility comes up often with leaders from industries of all stripes. In a column with Marla Malcolm Beck, the chief executive of Bluemercury, a beauty products and spa services retailer, she told Bryant that she limits her job interviews to seven to ten minutes and looks for three things: skill, will, and fit. "Will is about hunger," she said. "So I'll ask, 'What do you want to do in five or ten years?' That tells you a lot about their aspirations and creativity. If you're hungry to get somewhere, that means you want to learn. And if you want to learn, you can do any job."

2. Build an Expertise, Take Risks, and Learn the Meaning of Grit

If you watch college sports on television, you've probably seen the ad for Enterprise Rent-A-Car that features former college athletes behind the counter at your nearby Enterprise location. Enterprise—which hires more college graduates annually for entry-level management positions than any other company in the United States—likes to recruit college athletes as employees because they believe athletes know how to work on teams and multitask.

"We see a lot of transferable skills in athletes," Marie Artim, vice president of talent acquisition at Enterprise, told me.

Enterprise is not alone. As employers search for signals that someone is ready for a job beyond achieving the baseline bachelor's degree, participation in collegiate athletics is seen by many as one clear indicator of commitment and drive in a generation of college graduates often lacking both. Athletes are a textbook example of the ten thousand hours theory described by Malcolm Gladwell in his book *Outliers*—that it takes roughly ten thousand hours of practice to achieve mastery in a field. Athletes practice at all hours of the day and night, show up even when they don't feel like playing, and must have the drive to win. All are attributes important on the job. But athletes also come to the job with other experiences that recruiters told me are essential to success in the workplace: they've been reprimanded by a coach at some point for poor performance and they have overcome failure.

"They have a will to win," said Sarah Brubacher, head of eBay's university program, which has a special internship for former Olympic athletes. "That's what everyone needs to succeed."

This doesn't mean that employers are only interested in hiring jocks, of course. The qualities prized in athletes obviously apply to other college activities. Employers told me they value musicians, game designers, and writers in much the same way. The particulars of the activity don't matter as much as the time invested in the pursuit and mastery of the task.

"We want to see that they have a passion, and they show proficiency and go deep in it," said Adam Ward, head of recruiting at Pinterest, the popular online scrapbooking service. The advice I heard from Ward and other employers to go deep and not just broad runs counter to what high school guidance counselors preach when they encourage students to be "well-rounded."

The problem is that well-rounded students usually don't focus on any one thing for a prolonged period of time. Too often they seem to participate in activities just to check off a series of boxes instead of showing the deep and sustained involvement, passion, and dedication that employers seek. Their résumés are filled with what some recruiters refer to as "sign-up clubs." Well-rounded students typically turn into generalists on the job. While jack-of-all-trades were useful in previous generations, these days they are missing the critical expertise that makes up the vertical line of the T-shaped individual.

The more time students spend trying to master a skill or a job, the more likely they are to encounter failure. Recruiters repeatedly told me that today's college graduates don't have enough experience learning from failures or hardships, particularly on a job. Many of them didn't hold jobs in high school, working the register at McDonald's or folding clothes at the Gap like previous generations, and they are not skilled at prioritizing and dealing with the difficult clients that come with the rush of work.

"Our best employees are problem solvers and are able to weave everything they know together—customer service, empathy, persuasive skills, leadership skills, flexibility, and work ethic," Marie Artim of Enterprise told me. "They can think on their feet."

Enterprise has two hundred recruiters in the field who

actively recruit new employees on eight hundred college campuses each year. It has to work harder than most companies its size at attracting potential applicants among college students. After all, few people go to college with dreams of working for a rental-car company.

Despite its extensive outreach efforts, even Enterprise finds today's college graduates lacking in some basic skills, such as problem solving, decision making, and the ability to prioritize tasks. Too often new employees who are fresh out of college wait to be told what to do out of fear that they'll make the wrong decision. "This is a generation that has been 'syllabused' through their lives," Artim said. "Decisions were made for them, so we're less likely to find someone who can pull the trigger and make a decision."

Graduates can't simply flip a switch the day after college and start taking risks or learn to rebound from failures. These are behaviors we learn over time, and as a father of two young children, I see how our culture and schools instill a fear of failure beginning almost as soon as infants are able to walk. Like many parents, my wife and I wonder constantly whether we are building enough resilience in our children. Yet there we are with other parents at the neighborhood playground, watching over our children and ready to pounce in case one of them takes a tumble at the end of the slide.

"Children are born with the instinct to take risks in play, because historically, learning to negotiate risk has been crucial to survival," Hanna Rosin wrote in the April 2014 issue of the *Atlantic*. "But if they never go through that process, the fear can turn into a phobia." The story, titled "The Overprotected Kid," highlighted the evolution of the neighborhood playground as just one example in the daily lives of kids today where they are constantly supervised and, as a result, never find opportunities to take risks and perhaps fail.

What is unfortunate is that our desire to protect our kids and fill every waking moment of their schedules with organized activities seems only to worsen as they get older and receive a trophy merely for showing up at practice. And it doesn't stop in college. They pick their roommates in advance of arriving on campus. They live in apartment-like dorms, ensuring they basically never have to share a room or a bathroom, or even eat in the dining halls if they don't want to. Professors are encouraged to provide "trigger warnings," or advance notices to students that instructional material might elicit a troubling emotional response from them. And a handful of colleges have built electronic monitoring systems that encourage students to pick majors or courses where they are more likely to succeed (we'll take a closer look at these advising systems in Chapter 7).

The college campus has turned into one big danger-free zone. "Students used to come to me to get help solving a problem they had," a dean at one college told me. "Now they want me to just give them the answer."

The college classroom reinforces the message that failure is unacceptable. Students are never exposed, for instance, to the feedback process that is the hallmark of most jobs today. Think about it: employees don't work on a project in isolation for months and then turn it in to their boss just once at the end for feedback. There is a back-and-forth with small wins and many failures along the way. Even great writers discard several drafts. Yet in the college classroom, the sole focus of students is on the final product, whether an exam or a final paper, all done in an effort to earn an A. And that's exactly what many students end up getting. The A is the most common grade given out on college campuses nation-wide, accounting for 43 percent of all grades. (In 1988, the A represented less than one-third of all grades.) No wonder students are paralyzed by the prospect of failure—most of them have never experienced it.

When recruiters interview college students for jobs, they try to find applicants who have overcome challenges and learned from their disappointments. Some even give extra points to candidates whose personal stories exhibit that they have a certain fire in their belly.

Call it "grit"—a term used by Angela Duckworth, a psychology professor at the University of Pennsylvania. Her research has found that the most successful people are those not only with self-discipline but also with a singular determination to accomplish a task, no matter the obstacles. It's the deep passion Adam Ward at Pinterest told me his company looks for in employees.

To measure grit, Duckworth developed a simple twelve-question test that takes only a few minutes to complete, and it is remarkably accurate and increasingly used by companies and the military in assessing candidates (google the term "grit scale" to find it). When Duckworth gave it to more than 1,200 freshmen cadets at West Point as they entered a rigorous summer training course, the military found her test to be more predictive of which cadets would ultimately succeed than its own assessments.

Now the challenge for students—especially overly protected kids from high-achieving and high-income households—is to find relevant experiences that expose them to uncomfortable settings where they can learn from failure. You can no longer assume that it will come simply by going away to college. Unfortunately, the best lessons about taking risks and learning from failure often come on the very last day of college, via commencement speeches, when it's way too late.

3. Every Job Is a Tech Job

In a classroom tucked in a corner of Huntsman Hall, home to the Wharton School, the University of Pennsylvania's famed business school, Kevin Winters, an executive vice president at Caesars Entertainment, was talking about what it's like to work for the international gambling and entertainment conglomerate.

It was a rainy fall night, and the company was prepping a handful of Penn students for interviews the next day for its analytics team, a unit of 160 people based in Las Vegas who study customer behaviors for the marketing department. Its job involves analyzing complex data sets to achieve a simple goal: determine what will motivate Caesars' best customers to spend more money.

Framed by a PowerPoint presentation, Winters told the group of fifteen students that the company hires about two dozen people a year for the analytics team by recruiting at about twenty top universities. In the past, Caesars hired people for marketing positions who had a background and passion for hospitality. Now these are mostly data-driven jobs and require a whole new skill set. Marketing majors without the ability to understand algorithms fail to make the cut.

"You'll be able to work with the smartest people," Winters told the group. "It doesn't matter what your major is."

Even so, I suspected that these undergraduates and graduates in the room were mostly business majors. But a quick poll revealed that about half the students were actually humanities majors. "The great thing about an English degree is that you can do just about anything if you have analytical ability to go along with writing and communications skills," a student named Monica told me.

Indeed, the last decade has seen the rise of the "digital humanities," a combination of classic humanities disciplines and computing. This has opened up new jobs and careers for graduates in data visualization, digital mapping, and curating online collections. The same is true in journalism, where reporters who can manipulate massive databases to discover stories and illustrate anecdotes with solid statistics are in constant demand by news organizations. And other careers are quickly following, if they haven't already. Data-driven skills in a variety of occupations are the future.

Call it the new liberal arts, where digital awareness is just as important as rhetoric, writing, and critical thinking. No wonder liberal arts colleges are adding computer science classes and majors. It's no longer good enough to know how to use a computer.

Understanding the programming language behind the apps on your iPhone or the basics of artificial intelligence is now seen as basic foundational skills by many employers. Learning to program is much like learning a second language was in the twentieth century: you might not become proficient enough to move overseas, but you could get by if you traveled to a particular country.

"It's more about giving people the skills and tools they learn in the act of coding," Carol Smith, who oversees Google's Summer of Code program, told *Wired* magazine. "It gives them the critical thinking skills that are important whether or not they go into computer science as a profession."

The National Science Foundation estimates that 1.4 million jobs in the future will require computing skills. But less than a quarter of high school students take a coding class by the time they graduate and only 10 percent of high schools even offer college-level courses in computing.

"Every major company today has been transformed into a technology company," Brian Fitzgerald said. Fitzgerald heads up the Business-Higher Education Forum, an organization that brings together senior business and university executives, so he hears early on if there is a disconnect between what the economy needs and what the higher education system is producing. "Even non-tech jobs are tech jobs," Fitzgerald told me.

More than a decade ago, when financial transactions were becoming more complicated and competitive, the banking sector was the first industry to realize that being tech savvy was crucial for all employees. Banks were able to attract STEM (science, technology, engineering, and math) majors away from other industries with offers of big paychecks, leaving other companies scrambling to find talent among those who were left.

Fitzgerald told me that the big need now is for expertise in cybersecurity. And again, companies are looking for employees across a range of departments who, as Fitzgerald put it, are cyber-aware. "If you're in the sales department or communications department at Northrop Grumman, you have to understand the basics of cybersecurity even if it's not your job every day," Fitzgerald said.

The generation entering college and the workforce now are often referred to as "digital natives" because they were raised on technology from a very young age. But their relationship has been largely passive: switch on the device and use it. Being digitally aware isn't about turning more people into computer geeks. It's about moving from a passive relationship with technology to a more active one—especially in understanding the how and why behind machines, not just the what.

4. Learn to Deal with Ambiguity

Three months after I graduated from college, and following a summer journalism fellowship at the *Arizona Republic* in Phoenix, I had my first interview for a full-time newspaper reporting job. It was in Wilmington, North Carolina. The managing editor of the newspaper picked me up at the airport, and after a quick lunch, he dropped me off on Front Street, the historic main thoroughfare along the banks of the Cape Fear River. He told me to go find a story.

It was a Friday afternoon in late August, and I had to report and write the story by five P.M. I had never been to Wilmington before, and I didn't know anyone else in town. I didn't have a car. All I had was the notepad and pen the editor kindly gave me. For the next several hours, I roamed the streets talking to business owners, local residents, and tourists.

I eventually found a story—about a tourism campaign the state was undertaking after a close call with a hurricane—and filed it on time. But as the editor later told me, the article itself was not the test. It was my reaction when he dropped me off: he wanted to see what I would do in an unfamiliar situation. Other job candidates, he said, panicked and asked for a specific assignment, or they figured out how to get the job done. He wanted employees who could cope with the unknown on a daily basis.

As artificial intelligence increasingly makes many jobs obsolete, success in the future will belong to those able to tolerate ambiguity in their work. Too many recent graduates, however, approach their job descriptions the way they did a syllabus in college—as a recipe for winning in a career. They want concrete, well-defined tasks, as if they were preparing for an exam in college.

"Excelling at any job is about doing the things you weren't asked to do," said Mary Egan, founder of Gatheredtable, a Seattle-based start-up, and former senior vice president for strategy and corporate development at Starbucks. "This generation is not as comfortable with figuring out what to do."

I met Egan at a program for recent college graduates looking for help in launching their careers. She encouraged the unemployed graduates to take on more than just what would be listed in their job descriptions, particularly the minor tasks that eat up time for their bosses. "The more you can do to clear off your boss's plate and free up his or her days, the more valuable you become to the organization," Egan said. But she also told them to know their boundaries: too many twentysomethings believe they should be the one running the company or deserve a promotion three months after they start an entry-level job (more on humility later).

Like many of the other twenty-first-century skills sought by employers, a tolerance for ambiguity is often developed early in life. The feedback children get from adults and teachers has an enormous impact on their ability to deal with uncertainty. Carol Dweck, a Stanford University psychology professor, has found that praising children for their intelligence, rather than for their effort, often leads them to give up when they encounter the unknown. It's much better, in her opinion, to compliment children for their persistence. People perform better when they can focus on things they can control rather than things they cannot.

" 'Hard working' is what gets the job done," Dweck said. "The students who thrive are not necessarily the ones who come in with the perfect scores. It's the ones who love what they're doing and go at it vigorously."

Dweck has conducted several studies over the years that found that people would do better if they thought of their intelligence as flexible and not something fixed at birth. People who have what she calls a "growth mind-set" see challenges as opportunities to broaden their skills. But people who have been constantly praised for their intelligence freeze in ambiguous situations when they don't know the answer and often tie themselves in knots trying to reach perfection.

When I interviewed for that reporting job in North Carolina, I had no clue how much journalism would evolve over the coming decades. Even so, the set of skills journalism provided me—particularly the initiative to find a story every day, the ability to recognize patterns and trends, and to synthesize disparate ideas—remain invaluable no matter what I do. You don't need to major in journalism or become a reporter, of course, to acquire that set of skills, but those skills are crucial to navigating a future workplace marked with so much uncertainty.

The ability to negotiate ambiguity on the job requires people to think contextually, to provide what I call the "connective tissue" that occupies the space in between ideas. It is the "killer app" of today's workplaces. People who make these connections do so by following their curiosity and exploring and learning from peers. Knowledge is not only what is in our brains, but also what is distributed throughout our networks. Learning happens by building and navigating those networks.

But these networks are not just virtual—places such as Facebook, Twitter, Snapchat, or LinkedIn. Some of the best connections between knowledge occur in face-to-face conversations. As an editor at the *Chronicle of Higher Education,* I found that interns and young reporters too often relied on e-mail or Facebook for their reporting instead of simply picking up the phone or leaving the office to talk to a real human being. Managers in other industries told me the same thing: there is a need for more human interaction in a day and age when everyone has his or her head down, texting on smartphones.

"The art of conversation remains a powerful learning tool," John Leutner of Xerox reminded me.

Employers are trying to better measure during the interview process how job applicants learn and adapt to new situations. Take Google, one of the most difficult places in the world for new graduates to land a job. Until 2010, it required all potential candidates to provide SAT scores, scores on their graduate admissions exams if they had them, and college transcripts. "It was a ridiculous requirement," Laszlo Bock, who is the senior vice president of people operations at Google (a fancy title for head of human resources), told me. "What value did we possibly see in knowing just one dimension of a person, often from years earlier?"

The answer was none. Google came to realize that if test scores were any kind of predictor for performance, it was limited to the first two or three years after college. So it stopped asking for test scores, except when the applicant was a brand-new graduate. Instead, Bock said, Google began to rely on other measures it developed to assess how candidates solve knotty problems in real life.

It tested candidates by asking them to perform some of the actual work they'd do on the job. This is a popular technique consulting firms use, where interviews often include case studies. After being provided with just a few details (as when my editor dropped me off in the middle of town to find a story), candidates are asked to provide advice to a struggling company. Google also developed a test of general cognitive ability, a simple IQ test.

"Cognitive ability includes the capacity to learn," Bock said. "The combination of intelligence and learning ability is what makes people successful in most jobs."

5. Be Humble and Learn from Your Peers and Mentors

It was the first day of the summer internship at a major cereal company. One of the new interns told her boss at a meeting that she had invented a new cereal, complete with a box design and the recipe. Forget about the boring data-entry project she'd been assigned for the summer; this precocious college student wanted to know when she could present her idea to senior executives. "The sooner the better," she told her boss.

That's a story told by Bruce Tulgan in *Not Everyone Gets a Trophy: How to Manage Generation Y,* and it's similar to tales I heard from other people who manage recent college graduates. They all had the same complaint about their new hires: they're too impatient about their careers and unrealistic about their roles within a company.

A friend who is my age and a manager at a major media company told me about new graduates who applied for senior roles after less than a year on the job and who were then flabbergasted when they didn't get the promotion, which went to someone with ten or twenty years more experience. Of course, adults have long groused about "kids these days," but the concerns I heard came from a range of managers, even those who have been hiring new college graduates for decades.

One tech company executive told me of a recent graduate who asked for an opportunity to develop new products. When the company suggested a "hackathon" with a specific theme—to build an app for new hires—this employee proposed working on other business ideas instead and wanted to be sure she would own the rights to whatever she started. "We said it was our intellectual property, and she said it wasn't fair," the executive relayed. "It was all about what we could do for her."

Recent college graduates are largely conditioned to avoid

failure or didn't hold part-time jobs in high school where they might have worked with people of different ages and perspectives, so they often come to the workplace after college much more self-confident—some might say cocky—than previous generations did.

But being socially aware goes beyond knowing your role within the organization. It includes important skill sets like written and verbal communication as well as the ability to deal with negative feedback, speak in public, and, most of all, interact on a basic human level with coworkers and clients that doesn't involve texting them. While researching this book, recruiters shared with me plenty of examples of e-mail messages that they received from prospective job candidates that were unusually casual in their tone ("Hi Joe . . .") and, in some cases, incomprehensible.

To help this new generation of graduates transition to the world of work, many companies have recognized that they need to add training opportunities to their usual lineup of orientation classes. The giant online marketplace eBay is one of them. It has a weeklong hands-on orientation where new college graduates work in teams to come up with business ideas to help the company's products better appeal to millennials. It also offers classes on managing your personal brand (because new graduates usually can't set goals for themselves), giving an elevator pitch (they often can't get to their point fast enough), managing your calendar (once again, time management), and performance reviews.

Sarah Brubacher of eBay told me that students who grew up in a grading system of A through F often can't handle receiving a 3 on a 1 to 5 scale in a review. "That means they've met expectations," Brubacher said. "If you're meeting expectations, it means you're doing a great job, but for many high-achieving students, they see that as a C."

Why Are Employers Unhappy?

IN SURVEY AFTER SURVEY, EMPLOYERS SAY THAT TODAY'S college graduates are missing the broad attributes they seek most in a fast-changing economy. There remains a wide disconnect between how ready students say they are and what employers really think of them.

One pair of 2015 surveys of soon-to-be graduates and employers found that, on a range of nearly twenty skills, employers consistently rated students much lower than they judged themselves. While 57 percent of students said they were creative and innovative, for example, only 25 percent of employers agreed.

A wide gulf also exists between college leaders and business executives on the subject of job readiness for today's college graduates. Nearly all the chief academic officers who responded to a Gallup survey in 2014 said they were confident they prepared their graduates to be successful in the workplace. To them, the issue was one of demand—there were not enough jobs for their graduates. For employers, though, the issue was one of supply—colleges may be producing enough graduates, but not enough of them had the right set of skills. Just 11 percent of business leaders said that colleges prepared their graduates to be successful in the workplace.

Assessment tests of college graduates seem to support the view of employers. One test administered to 32,000 students at 169 colleges and universities in 2015 found that 40 percent of college seniors did not possess the complex reasoning skills needed in today's workplace. The Collegiate Learning Assessment Plus (CLA+), given to freshmen and seniors, measures the gains made during college in critical thinking, writing and communication, and analytical reasoning. Its results found little difference between those students who graduated from public colleges and those who went to private schools.

Not surprisingly, students who graduated from the best colleges did better than everyone else on the test as seniors, but their gains after taking the test as freshmen were actually smaller than those of students who graduated from less elite schools. The big difference in the results depended on the college major: students who studied math and science scored significantly higher than those who studied in the so-called helping and service fields, such as social work, or in business, which is the most popular college major.

Such assessments and surveys should put students on alert—you may think you are ready for a career with a college degree, especially one from a prestigious school, but many employers think otherwise. It is becoming clear that the most successful graduates in the job market are acquiring the broad range of skills employers want outside the classroom and the normal channels of college, and sometimes they're taking longer than the traditional four-year timeline to do so. Indeed, if you're unsure what you want to do or lack many of the skills outlined above, perhaps the best way to launch into adulthood is to slow down the conveyor belt you're on through college. Take time off before you arrive on campus or during your undergraduate years to find your interests, explore your career options, and bolster the skills needed to succeed in the workplace.

CHAPTER 3

THE BENEFITS OF A DETOUR

T HE SUMMER AFTER I GRADUATED FROM HIGH SCHOOL, I WORKED AT THE LOCAL BRANCH OF AAA. MY JOB WAS TO PRODUCE "TRIPTIKS" FOR its members—personalized directions to a specific destination, neatly packaged in a spiral-bound notebook that allowed drivers to flip a page every fifty miles or so and follow the highlighted roads. The notebooks always included state maps in case drivers wanted to explore something new or perhaps discover a different way to their final destination. This was before GPS in our cars and on our smartphones made these paper TripTiks and foldout maps obsolete. Now a faceless computer tells us where to go, and we all follow the same roads to get from point A to point B the fastest. Most of us rarely venture off course and look for alternative, perhaps more interesting, routes.

The same is true for emerging adults in their pathway

from high school to college to the start of their career. They follow a well-plotted and well-trod course beginning a short three months after high school graduation and go along with the pack because they don't know what else to do.

They often select a major before they even step foot in their first class on a campus. "What's your major going to be?" is the second question eighteen-year-olds are asked right after "Where are you going to college?" No wonder so many teenagers think that choosing a major is like deciding on a career for life (it's not).

This track leads many teenagers to pick careers based on what is familiar to them, not necessarily what they might be passionate about. If their neighbors or parents or friends' parents are doctors, lawyers, and teachers, they will likely choose one of those paths as well. With many occupations found primarily in only certain regions—tech jobs, for example, are largely concentrated along the coasts—swaths of students have no exposure to careers that might interest them.

There must be a better way to help teenagers locate the on-ramp to college, a career, and eventually a purposeful life.

The decades-long march to college-for-everyone at eighteen has actually closed off rather than opened up options for teenagers and twentysomethings. As recently as the 1970s, a teenager had a number of options after graduating from high school: get a good-paying job right away, enlist in the military, find an apprenticeship in a trade, or go to college. A teenager today really has only two of those options still available: the military or college. Less than 1 percent of Americans serve in the military, so most go to college right after high school. In the early 1970s, less than half of high school graduates in the United States went on to college the following fall. Today, nearly 66 percent do.

If emerging adults are to succeed eventually in the job market, they need environments where they can explore for a while before they settle. The family home and high school, with their close supervision and regimented schedule, don't provide such space.

So what would happen if tens of thousands of recent high school graduates took time off *before* they went to college to explore careers, work and earn money, learn new skills? Could it lead to more of them sticking with college later on, and after graduation moving more quickly into a job and career? What if college students took time off *during* school or *right after* graduation to engage in the world around them, to test out a business idea or get the job they never had in high school because they were too worried about going to the right college? Would they better navigate the early part of their career and gain the soft skills that employers want and colleges too often fail to provide?

General Stanley McChrystal thinks so. He's the former commander of U.S. and international forces in Afghanistan and has witnessed firsthand the benefits of military service for teenagers and twentysomethings. He now leads the Aspen Institute's Franklin Project, which has a goal to create 1 million civilian national-service positions for young adults.

"There's this rush to figure out what you're going to do," McChrystal said. "We have cultlike expectations to get started in life because you don't want to fall behind. Life is not linear. Neither should the pathways of getting started."

The Benefits of Taking Time Off

SABRINA SKAU WAS ABOUT TO HEAD STRAIGHT INTO COL-
lege in 2007. But a few weeks before she had to pack up for
her first year at the University of Rochester, she realized she
wasn't as excited about going as her friends. For Sabrina, this
was more than the typical teenage anxiety about moving
across the country for school. The University of Rochester
wasn't her first choice. She was burned out from academics
in high school and felt like she was going to college only
because it was expected of her.

"It was what I was supposed to do next," she said. "You
graduate from high school and then you go to college. My
parents had never discussed not going."

Sabrina's parents also noticed she wasn't thrilled with her
choice. They suggested she take some time off—a gap year
between high school and college—and she jumped at the
chance (something Valerie the Wanderer from Chapter 1
never broached with her parents). Sabrina's parents reached
out to Holly Bull, a well-known gap-year consultant whose
father, back in the 1980s, helped popularize the concept of
a break before college. Bull connected Sabrina to a program
in Costa Rica where she could teach English. A few weeks
later, instead of packing up for college in Upstate New York,
Sabrina left for Central America.

"The gap year is a jewel that comes one time in life, allowing you to step away and get a good read on who you
really are," said Bull. She was addressing a group of parents
and students in an auditorium at Thomas S. Wootton High

School in Rockville, Maryland, just outside of Washington, D.C. It was a cold, blustery February night, during yet another competitive college admissions season at Wootton, where 95 percent of graduates go right on to college. Still, the auditorium was packed with students looking for some other route.

I was at a gap-year fair, one of nearly fifty held at high schools around the country every winter, during which several dozen providers of gap-year experiences exhibit their programs to prospective students. It had the look and the feel of a traditional college fair, except more parents were there. Many were skeptical about even being there. After all, they had spent more than eighteen years preparing to send their kids immediately off to college following high school.

After Bull's talk, the crowd headed to the downstairs cafeteria, and in the stairway, I overheard a cacophony of opinions about Bull's pitch. Though a few parents wished they had been offered a gap year in their day, I mostly heard worry in their voices—about the cost, over deferring or rejecting a seat at a top university ("But what about *Stanford*?" one father pleaded with his daughter), and whether a gap year would put these eighteen-year-olds behind in college and, eventually, in the job market.

In the cafeteria, the gap-year companies lined up behind long tables, one after another displaying giant posters of exotic locations—photos of students helping children in a third-world country or, closer to home, a whitewater rafting trip down the Colorado River. I felt I had wandered into a travel convention. Most gap programs at fairs like this one have a travel component, like Sabrina's experience teaching English in Costa Rica. In theory, taking teenagers outside their familiar territory builds resilience. It also adds to the price tag, which can sometimes soar to upward of $20,000 for six months, giving the gap year a reputation as a club for rich kids to go backpacking through Europe or to do good in an African village.

The stereotype stems partly from the roots of the gap year in the eighteenth-century Grand Tour, when British men from privileged backgrounds traveled around Europe to explore art, history, and culture. Even today, an estimated two hundred thousand students in the United Kingdom defer admission to a university to travel or work. There are no comparable statistics for the United States, but judging from the attendance at fairs like this one, the idea is growing in popularity. At the same time, more and more gap-year providers are trying to appeal to middle- and low-income students.

Sure, gap years are expensive, but in some cases an investment in a year off might be money saved later on if students are more directed when they eventually go to college. After all, four out of ten students who start at four-year colleges don't earn a degree after *six* years.

Colleges are opening up to the idea of time off as well, even considering the gap year as a built-in feature of the first year—a freshman year spent off campus, working, exploring careers, taking classes, or traveling (although usually not for academic credit). A decade-plus ago, the dean of admissions at Harvard University wrote a seminal essay in the *New York Times* encouraging high school graduates to take a year off. "It is a time to step back and reflect, to gain perspective on personal values and goals, or to gain needed life experience in a setting separate from and independent of one's accustomed pressures and expectations," William R. Fitzsimmons wrote.

For years, Harvard's acceptance letters included a suggestion that students consider taking a break. But here the college's head of admissions was actively lobbying for the idea of a gap year, and that caused a niche concept to get much more attention. Over the next decade, Harvard saw a 33 percent jump in the number of students taking a gap year. Dozens of other colleges and universities began advertising the option on their websites.

Still, plenty of parents and students remain unconvinced that gap years are beneficial. Guidance counselors, who are usually evaluated by how many students they send right on to college, rarely recommend a gap year. Parents worry their kids will take a permanent detour and skip college altogether.

Some parents admire the concept but aren't quite sure it's right for all their children. One parent whose daughter took a gap year told me that she would never suggest it to her sons. In her mind, boys need more structure. There is plenty of research on how boys are falling behind girls academically, so a gap year to mature and let their frontal lobes better connect with their brains might be exactly what many boys need. Women are more likely to start and finish college. Some 70 percent of women enroll in college and 46 percent of them complete a degree, while 61 percent of men start college and only 39 percent finish. Research has found that parents seem more willing to send their daughters, rather than their sons, to higher-priced schools because they think girls are the better bet when it comes to getting a degree.

Every year, about 20 percent of high school graduates delay college for some period of time, about half of them for just a year. But not all time off from education is created equal. The reasons high school graduates put off college are critically important to how well they eventually do in school and in their career.

For the gap year to truly matter, it can't be simply a break, a year spent sleeping in your childhood bedroom and working part-time at McDonald's. Students who delay college to work odd jobs for a while to try to "find themselves" don't do as well as everyone else when they get to campus. They get lower grades and there's a greater chance they will drop out.

But students whose gap years involve travel—whether to a foreign country or to a different part of the United States—not only end up with higher grades in college, but they also graduate at the same rate as those who don't delay at all.

In other words, taking a short break for a structured gap year has a positive impact on academic performance and doesn't take students off track in getting their start in life, a big worry of parents I meet. Indeed, research has found that when gap-year students arrive on campus, they take their studies more seriously and don't engage in risky behavior, such as alcohol abuse.

For a gap year to have a significant impact on your success in college, and later in the working world, it needs to be a transformative event, quite distinct from anything you have experienced before. It should also be designed to help you acquire the skills and attributes that colleges and employers are looking for: maturity, confidence, problem solving, communication skills, and independence.

Traditionally, the gap year has been defined as time off before college, but the benefits of taking time off are usually the same whether you're about to head off to school, you're in college, or about to start your career. Whatever time period you choose, you should consider one of three different approaches when structuring the year off: it needs to either yield *meaningful work experience, academic preparation for college,* or *travel that opens up the horizon to the rest of the world.*

Let's take a closer look at how students navigate those three routes when taking time off.

The Travel Gap Year

Abby Falik grew up in Berkeley, California, across the bay from San Francisco. She knew during her senior year in high school, even as she was applying to colleges, that she needed a break from school. At age sixteen, she had spent a summer in a Nicaraguan village, and it inspired in her a hunger for learning in a different culture. She called the Peace Corps to apply for an overseas assignment. "They turned me down because I didn't have a college degree," she told me one morning when we met for coffee near her office in Oakland.

Falik followed her original plan and enrolled at Stanford. As she had predicted, she was antsy sitting in classrooms listening to professors talk about international development, when what she longed for instead was to apply what she was learning. After finishing her sophomore year, she took a year off to travel to Nicaragua and Brazil to set up a library and work with a nonprofit.

"It was the most challenging and most formative time of my life," she said, although she didn't receive any academic credits for her experience.

Falik eventually came to realize that her year overseas occurred at the wrong time in her undergraduate career because it was too late to change what she had done her first two years in college. What was true for her is probably true for others who go abroad while in college. Nearly three hundred thousand American students study in a foreign country each year. Most do so in their junior year. Falik wondered if studying abroad would have a bigger impact on how students approached college if they traveled *before* their freshman year instead of waiting until they were almost done with school.

After graduating from Stanford in 2001 and working at various nonprofits, Falik ended up at Harvard Business School. In 2008, while a student there, she won first place in a pitch competition for new social enterprises. Her plan: a global "bridge year" before college. A year later, her idea became reality with Global Citizen Year, a nonprofit that gives high school graduates a gap year working in a developing country.

Falik is in her late thirties with shoulder-length dark hair and a blissful smile as a fairly new mom. She corrected me when I called Global Citizen Year a "gap year." To her, the metaphor is a poor marketing strategy, especially for today's parents who are worried about their kids getting off track on the way to a career. She wants to rebrand the break as a "bridge year" or a "launch year," and hopes to make the experience the norm in the United States, not the exception for just a select group of students. In another decade, she aims to have ten thousand students enrolled annually in Global Citizen Year.

Falik's enthusiasm for a universal transition year before college is infectious. She has already signed up several schools as partners. Tufts University has added Global Citizen Year as an option for incoming students, who pay $33,000 for the experience. The provost there told me he could imagine half the class arriving via that route one day, although students would still have to complete the traditional four years on the Tufts campus near Boston.

Universities have tremendous financial incentive not to cut the four-year residential experience short. Of course, that policy doesn't help students. I asked Falik what it would take to make the bridge year *the* first year of college for everyone, where students get credit for their time off so that they don't spend yet more time and money on earning their bachelor's degree. She mentioned the same cultural barriers everyone else described to me—the education conveyor belt that's almost impossible to stop.

"Until we stop thinking that the best solution is to go from school to more school, we're not going to succeed," she said.

Even as the idea of the gap year expands beyond its roots, travel remains the most popular option for how students spend their time off, and for good reason. Travel is a powerful learning tool for emerging adults. It requires them to ask questions and engage with others who are different, to reflect on the scenes they are seeing, and, perhaps most of all, to adapt to new languages, cultures, and food.

Researchers have found that college students who take the time to reflect and connect course material to their prior experiences, knowledge from other activities, and the wider world are more engaged in college and can better navigate their lives. But only a quarter of freshmen say their colleges encourage such deeper reflection that leads to their growth, and the proportion is only slightly higher among college seniors.

"Teenagers have a way of being stuck in a certain way of

doing things, and you can't do that when you're traveling," said Sabrina, who spent her gap year in Costa Rica. "Things constantly get thrown at you, and you need to figure it out without much help."

Near the end of her gap year, Sabrina was accepted to Brown University, where she had been wait-listed a year earlier. Her year away likely made her a stronger applicant at Brown. At the very least, the year gave her clarity about her major (anthropology), improved her Spanish, and taught her to relax about where she'd go to college.

"I had lived inside of myself for so long prior to going on my gap year," said Sabrina, who is now working in documentary and film production in Los Angeles while pursuing a master's degree.

When I talked with other students who traveled during their gap year, I heard many similar stories. The year helped them decide what they really wanted to major in (usually not what they had originally picked). It gave them perspective about their place in the world, particularly with the obsession most of them had about their academic performance. And it encouraged them to take more risks.

Ada Rauch, who spent a year in India in 2012 as part of a tuition-free gap year that Princeton offered, told me that she had never been outside the United States before. She was nervous to be far from home for so long, but the time working on service projects and taking classes helped her to get comfortable with risk, tolerate ambiguity, and become more resilient.

"I'm more open to new opportunities and seek out adventure that I didn't before," said Ada, who switched her major from physics to Near Eastern studies. She also no longer cared about her grades as much as her classmates who arrived directly from high school. "When I get a bad grade, I don't freak out," she said. "I know it doesn't matter in the larger scheme of things."

The Academic Gap Year

Wes Moore is Abby Falik's kindred spirit on the East Coast. In 2010, Moore wrote a bestselling book, *The Other Wes Moore,* that told the story of two African American kids with difficult childhoods who grew up blocks apart in Baltimore. One went on to graduate from Johns Hopkins University and became a Rhodes Scholar and a decorated army veteran, while the other ended up serving a life sentence in prison for murder. I met the Rhodes Scholar Moore for lunch soon after he released his book.

Moore is well known in Baltimore and a mentor to many young people. Those interactions have contributed to his belief that there is a missing piece in the transition after high school, a program that can help the kids better prepare for college.

Moore has an athletic build from his days of playing football in college and speaks in a calm and soothing voice. Like Falik, he is part of a new generation of social entrepreneurs attempting to reinvent the gap year for today's students who come from a much wider range of academic and economic backgrounds than those of three decades ago. And like Falik, he roots his idea for a gap year in his own autobiography: he transferred to Johns Hopkins after a bridge year at a military school.

To him, the traditional gap year is not only too expensive for low- and middle-income students, but it isn't focused enough on academics at a time when many students need extra help to get ready for college. According to the testing service ACT, almost a third of high school graduates are not prepared academically for first-year college courses. Moore wanted to build a gap year that combined four elements: college courses, work, career exploration through internships, and, most important, a total price tag under $8,000. He called it "a gap year for all."

Without an academic component to a gap year, Moore worried that struggling students would allow the skills they developed in high school to deteriorate even further during the break and lose interest in going to college at all.

A few years later, Moore invited me to Baltimore for the graduation of his first class of BridgeEdU. The vision he laid out for me was now mostly a reality. The graduation was held on the top floor of the law offices of Peter Angelos, the owner of the Baltimore Orioles baseball team.

One of the graduates, Chanel Whisonant, told me she had earned eighteen credits during her gap year that she planned to take with her to a four-year university, either Morgan State or Coppin State, in Maryland. She said the year off had allowed her to gain the confidence she needed to succeed in college.

In BridgeEdU, she took only two classes each semester, allowing her to focus on her deficiencies instead of having the distractions of the full load of five courses she probably would have taken in her freshman year of college. "The teachers were very willing to work with you, not like high school," she said. She also had an internship at the National Aquarium in Baltimore's Inner Harbor and worked closely with academic coaches during her year off. People in the program, she said, "believed in me when I didn't believe in myself."

Students who are not ready for college right after high school—either academically or emotionally—are not helped in the long run by being pushed and prodded to enroll in college. But parents, teachers, and counselors continue to do it, and it isn't any wonder that so many students come to college campuses unprepared and with only vague ideas about why they are really there. Studies conducted by the psychologist William Damon found that only one in five young people has a clear vision of what they want to accomplish in life.

Many more arrive on campus totally unprepared for their courses. About half of students at community colleges and 20 percent of those at four-year colleges are placed in remedial courses, essentially do-over high school classes, which don't count toward their graduation requirements. Many of them skip the classes, or don't pass the courses, get discouraged, and eventually drop out of college. Just a little more than one-third of students who take remedial courses at four-year colleges graduate within six years.

A year off before college that combines a few courses with meaningful work could spark the academic turnaround that many of those students desperately need and a sense of focus they previously lacked.

A Gap Year to Explore Meaningful Work

AmeriCorps is probably the closest thing the United States has to a national gap year. This national-service program was a campaign promise Bill Clinton made while running for president in 1992 and was begun during his first year in office.

AmeriCorps never reached the yearly five hundred thousand participants Clinton had wanted, mostly because the program has been perpetually underfunded, but that certainly is not for a lack of demand. Nearly six hundred thousand people apply for eighty thousand spots annually, only half of which are even full-time. Its wide variety of assignments range from cleaning up public lands and building houses to tutoring kids, making it a perfect gap-year experience for students unsure of what they want to do next in life.

That was true for Ryeshia Farmer when she graduated from high school in Milwaukee in 2012. She was working at Burger King to save money for college but didn't want to spend her savings until she had a better sense of what was next for her. She applied to City Year, which receives funding from AmeriCorps and places young people like her in schools around the country to tutor students. Some 2,700 students are selected from 13,000 applicants to participate in the program each year, an acceptance rate that rivals that of many selective colleges.

Ryeshia was accepted and was able to stay in Milwaukee to save money. She didn't travel like so many other students who choose to delay college, but she had a meaningful work experience that was quite different from anything she had ever done before. If you aren't able to travel during your time off, be sure to find an experience that is totally un-familiar and will force you to navigate through uncertain situations and perhaps even fail from time to time.

In Ryeshia's case, she worked alongside a variety of generations that helped her better understand specific career paths and the nuances of the workplace. Ryeshia helped teach a group of students in math and reading during the school day and gave them additional help following classes. She also helped coordinate after-school programs for City Year in the Milwaukee area.

"It was a complex position for anyone my age," she said. "At Burger King, a computer tells you what order is up next. It's mindless. At City Year, I had to structure my day, make independent decisions, manage competing priorities, and then change on the fly."

Ryeshia started at Carthage College in Wisconsin the next fall, and, like other gap-year participants I interviewed, she found that the year off had helped her figure out what was next for her. (Or not, because Ryeshia decided she definitely didn't want to be a teacher.) None of the gap-year students who took time off before college ever considered skipping school altogether.

Even so, about half of students who delay college right after high school do so for *more than* one year. One of the biggest issues facing those who want to take time off before or during college is how long the break should last. Some sort of education after high school is absolutely necessary in today's economy, but where and when that education is acquired is a question more students should ask themselves before simply following the road from high school to college without knowing what they want to get out of their undergraduate years.

The Permanent Gap Year

"SKIP COLLEGE, START A TECHNOLOGY COMPANY" HAS become a popular refrain in recent years, and some of its biggest proponents have come from the ranks of Silicon Valley entrepreneurs—even though they often went to college themselves and usually send their own kids there (typically to the best ones).

The loudest among the advocates for this is Peter Thiel, who made billions as a founder of PayPal and an investor in Facebook. In 2010, at an annual conference for start-ups in San Francisco, Thiel announced a gap year that he hoped would become a permanent break: he would give $100,000 each to a small group of smart young adults, many of whom were already undergraduates at the nation's elite colleges, to skip out on school and do something else. He told the largely sympathetic crowd that higher education was too expensive, encouraged conformity, and failed to teach entrepreneurship.

"We need to be spending a lot more time focusing on the kinds of breakthrough technologies that will take our civilization to the next level," he said.

His talk became one of those galvanizing moments in the history of higher education, coming at a time of economic uncertainty, high student loan debt for college graduates, and the fundamental questioning of the value of a bachelor's degree. Thiel initially wanted to create a new university through his foundation to further his vision, but he concluded that "to compete within the system would be tremendously expensive and probably futile."

As journalist Beth McMurtrie would later report in the *Chronicle of Higher Education,* most of the initial class of "Thiel Fellows" moved on from their original ideas for start-ups, and a few who had dropped out of college ended up going back to school. The fellowship was "an awesome opportunity to learn something about what we love doing and maybe challenge ourselves," said Daniel Friedman, who abandoned an e-commerce company after the fellowship and now is a partner in a new company. "And if a year or two later we messed everything up, we could go back to school."

That's the difference with taking a detour like a gap year early in life: it's easy to find an on-ramp back to your original route. Nothing is permanent when you don't have the obligations of adulthood.

Perhaps the most well known Thiel fellow is Dale Stephens, who dropped out of Hendrix College in Arkansas after seven months, wrote a book called *Hacking Your Education,* and is now the self-appointed leader of the UnCollege movement, an effort in self-directed learning. For $16,000, he offers his own version of a gap year that combines living abroad, workshops, an internship, and personal coaching sessions. "We took the best part of what college does for you—the experiences you get outside the classroom—and said you don't need to spend four years and $60,000 a year to get it," Stephens told me.

The real value of what Stephens and Thiel offer is exactly what other gap-year programs and colleges extend to students without being so explicit about it: connections. Several Thiel Fellows said the program's best part was the network that Thiel plugged them into. It allowed them to test their ideas, to raise money, and, when things didn't work out, to have a place to help land a new job or start another company. It's the safety net that many Wanderers in Chapter 1 didn't have because they lacked access to the kind of people that someone like Thiel could introduce them to.

For most American teenagers, college still provides the best social network for someone starting out, and the better the school, often the better the network. That's why students, and especially their parents, drive themselves crazy to get into Stanford or Penn or Harvard. It's not because the education is so much better at those places; it's because of the network students connect to, through the parents of their classmates, alumni, and eventually through the students themselves when they become alumni. Even college dropouts such as Bill Gates and Mark Zuckerberg depended on the social capital they built in their short time at Harvard to start Microsoft and Facebook, respectively.

The difference, compared with two or three decades ago, is that Americans' social networks are increasingly segregated by geography. In previous eras, good jobs were pretty much spread out among cities and regions across the country. Now the college educated are migrating to a relatively small number of metropolitan regions. The people who benefit the most from the economic rewards of what the futurist Richard Florida calls the "means migration" are those who live in these select cities—and perhaps most of all, as we'll examine in the next chapter, the students who go to college in such cities and regions.

CHAPTER 4

WHY A COLLEGE'S LOCATION MATTERS

I F YOU GLANCE AT A MAP OF THE NEARLY FIVE THOU-
SAND AMERICAN COLLEGES AND UNIVERSITIES, YOU'LL
NOTICE TWO THINGS. FIRST, MOST ARE CLUSTERED IN
the Northeast and the upper Midwest. Second, a surprising
number of them are located in small towns and out-of-the
way places.

The first growth spurt of American higher education
occurred in the nineteenth century, when the country's
population was concentrated in the East and Northeast. As
communities expanded, new colleges, some affiliated with
churches and others operated by the states to train teachers
for the public schools, were started to serve local populations. The establishment of public land-grant universities in
the 1860s created a whole new class of institutions, mainly
in rural areas, where there were wide-open spaces to build

campuses and where they could most serve the state's agricultural interests.

Going off to college in the past was seen as a time to focus on your intellectual and social development with other young adults cloistered on campuses tucked far away from the distractions of daily life. As the population migrated from farms to cities, college campuses didn't pick up and move with them. Instead, the schools turned into the economic and cultural hub of their towns.

But as time went on, the idea of being sheltered on campuses, far from internship and research opportunities, began to fall out of favor with a generation of students interested in both. Sweet Briar College in Virginia recognized this trend too late. In March 2015, the tiny women's college with only seven hundred students announced that it would go out of business at the end of the academic year. Sweet Briar had been suffering from declining student interest for years.

"We are 30 minutes from a Starbucks," lamented Sweet Briar's president, James F. Jones Jr., in an interview he gave soon after the announcement was made.

The accepted narrative about why Sweet Briar failed was that high school girls weren't interested in going to a women's college anymore. But the pithy line from President Jones about Starbucks illustrates perhaps an even more fundamental issue facing Sweet Briar and hundreds of other schools across the country: the remote locations of their campuses.

What's long been said about real estate is now true for colleges as well—location matters. Students and their parents have typically scrutinized a school's place on a map with regard to the surrounding amenities: Are there enough restaurants and bars? Is it close to the beach or the mountains? I'll never forget my mom's comment as we drove the last thirty miles into Ithaca, New York, the summer before my senior year of high school for a campus tour of Ithaca College: "Just *what* are you going to do here?"

But a college's location is about more than whether students can quickly grab a tall cappuccino before class. Even in a virtual age, when it is easy to connect with anyone anywhere, a college's physical place matters more than ever before to its graduates' ultimate success in the job market. As the importance of off-campus experiences increases, students at schools in out-of-the-way places—especially areas without strong regional or national brands or colleges without deep pockets—often struggle to find the kinds of internships and work experiences nearby that are necessary to gain the skills employers want.

That's not to say that high school students should cross off every rural or far-flung college from their list of potential schools, or if you're already at one of those schools, consider transferring. College towns such as Ithaca, or Lawrence, Kansas, or Charlottesville, Virginia, still offer plenty of off-campus learning in spite of their out-of-the-way locations. Some of the best colleges and universities in the country are in small towns: Williams in Massachusetts, Grinnell in Iowa, Cornell in New York, and Dartmouth in New Hampshire.

What's more, a few remote campuses have mitigated their less-than-desirable place in the world by opening programs and campuses in major cities. Cornell University, for example, is building a giant science and tech campus on New York City's Roosevelt Island.

I'm not telling you to skip that classic rural campus experience if that's what you want. If I had to do it again, I'd still attend Ithaca College, my undergraduate alma mater. But if you choose that small-town route, be prepared to spend extra time finding real-world work opportunities outside of school and in cities. Often that means you'll need to head off to a metro area for a semester or over the summer to get the most beneficial experiences.

Some of the "hottest" universities—those that have improved their reputations dramatically in recent years—are in metropolitan areas, because cities with diverse and innovative economies offer today's college students a constant churn of classroom learning and work experience throughout the year.

As the creative juices and financial rewards of the economy cluster around two to three dozen communities across the country, nearby colleges and their students are poised to be some of the biggest beneficiaries. The knowledge that flows back and forth between the local economy and higher ed fuels the growth of intellectual capital for both sides, providing students with unparalleled opportunities for research projects and internships and, eventually, good jobs after graduation (I'll look more closely at internships in the next chapter).

It wasn't always that way. As recently as three decades ago, plenty of urban universities suffered from bad reputations, hampered by surroundings with few amenities and high crime rates. Understandably, parents sent their kids to rural and suburban campuses that were safer.

This flight from the cities was enough to persuade a few

leading urban universities to reconsider the streets around them as extensions of their campuses. Probably the best example is the University of Pennsylvania, which in the late 1990s invested hundreds of millions of dollars in retail stores, a hotel, and a public school and encouraged university employees to buy homes in the neighborhood. The streets around Penn improved and so did the university's application numbers and rankings. Penn and other urban campuses were also helped as sectors of the economy converged around a handful of cities and regions—tech in San Francisco, finance in New York City, pharmaceuticals in Philadelphia, medical devices in Boston, and entertainment in Los Angeles—further cementing the brands of those campuses that catered to their hometown industries.

As you think about *where* to go to college, don't just check out campuses that are good for your recreational interests, proximity to family, or your social life. Too often lifestyle trumps academics when making the college decision. It's not that your college years shouldn't be fun, but focusing only on the social aspects of your surroundings rather than on building a network or lining up the right internships will make it difficult to launch a career afterward.

A decade or so ago at Tulane University, students flocked to New Orleans for its food, music, and famed French Quarter, but had little involvement with the local community otherwise. But after Hurricane Katrina forced the university to shut down for an entire semester in 2005, the city and Tulane became dependent on each other to fuel their collective recoveries.

Tulane shifted its academic focus to the city it had previously ignored, mandating that all undergraduates complete two courses in community service, for instance. The university's former president Scott Cowen told me that students started to venture into New Orleans for more than its nightlife, and in doing so, they recognized the value of the local economy to their own future careers.

"The city turned into our campus," Cowen said. Students interested in their surroundings for reasons other than partying began to enroll as a result. This sparked an economic renaissance for both New Orleans and Tulane, one that has also emerged on campuses in metro areas across the country over the last few decades, including my hometown of Washington, D.C.

The Emergence of the Modern Urban University

UNTIL RECENTLY, I LIVED A FEW BLOCKS FROM AMERICAN University's campus in the leafy northwest section of D.C. In my old neighborhood, the university's fleet of shuttle buses were ubiquitous, each emblazoned with a phrase about its students, faculty, or alumni: AU'S PASSIONATE STUDENTS LOG OVER 100,000 SERVICE HOURS EACH YEAR. AU FACULTY APPEAR IN THE NEWS EVERY 24 MINUTES. They were a daily reminder of how a place like AU uses its location in the nation's capital as a key selling point.

Late one afternoon near the end of the spring semester, I walked to AU's campus to meet with the university's provost, Scott Bass. As I crossed the campus, I noticed how open it was to the surrounding city sidewalks. Unlike Columbia or Harvard, which have gates around their urban campuses, there were no physical barriers here. The lack of any wall surrounding the campus is more than an architectural feature. It's a symbolic statement, Bass explained to me later.

"We see the city as our laboratory for our students," he said. "Being in D.C. is an enormous advantage for our students, in their interactions with faculty who are very connected to the broader community and to top thinkers."

An important part of going to college is building the foundation of a social and professional network you can use in starting your career. That network can be constructed at a college anywhere through classmates, professors, and alumni, but a school in a large community or metro area gives students opportunities to extend the network well beyond the campus. This wider network of contacts can provide even students at less prestigious colleges an extra boost in the job market that the name on the degree alone can't furnish.

American University is a good school, but it's not in the top tier of national universities. *U.S. News & World Report* considers AU second tier, ranking it at number seventy-one nationwide. But compared with similarly ranked schools outside of a major city or suburb, urban institutions such as AU have three broad advantages tied to their location.

The first is the type of faculty that schools in metro areas can more easily recruit. AU has a mix of renowned scholars with Ph.D.s who are attracted to Washington's intellectual and cultural life *and* top experts in their field who work full-time in D.C. and teach on the side. This kind of faculty, which teaches both theory and practice, is beneficial to students who want to apply classroom learning to the real world. Unfortunately, many elite universities that brag about the scholarly accomplishments of their Ph.D. faculty lack these "hybrid" professors who have actually worked outside of academia and can bring that experience to students.

Second, the diversity of the local economy can open up internship opportunities—84 percent of AU students intern at least *twice* before they graduate—but also gives undergraduates access to organizations that add a real-life spin to classroom projects. Every year, for example, students in an AU marketing class partner with a major D.C. company, such as Hilton, Honest Tea, and LivingSocial, to solve a business challenge the company faces. Many other colleges offer similar courses, but few at the undergraduate level work as closely with actual managers at a local company. AU's provost told me that such courses, like the hybrid faculty, give students an important mix of the practical arts and the liberal arts.

"Students are having the interdisciplinary experiences that D.C. and AU provide," Bass said, "and it's challenging their thinking."

The third advantage is your fellow classmates. A desirable location often attracts good students, and that helps a college's academic quality. Some of the most important learning that happens in college comes from your peers, so you want to be surrounded by people who give you different perspectives on life and careers.

Recent graduates I talked to often said their best leads for internships and jobs came from their classmates or students a year or two ahead of them. That's the network effect of college—and it is supercharged in an urban environment. As Edward Glaeser, an economist at Harvard and author of *Triumph of the City,* has said, cities attract smart people, and the more we are around them, the smarter and more creative we get.

What's more, when a school attracts students who are very engaged in their studies, with one another, and with the wider community, it helps the institution's finances in all sorts of ways. Moody's Investors Services, which examines the financial health of colleges, has been pessimistic about the higher education business in recent years. But it is bullish on urban institutions that are popular among students.

"Rural institutions are doing less well," Dennis Gephardt, a vice president at Moody's, told me. A quarter of regional public colleges—usually located in states' sparsely populated areas—have seen a decline in their net tuition revenue (the money they have left over after they give financial aid to students). Gephardt specifically pointed to American University as a school that has benefited from being located in the nation's capital and a few blocks from the more prestigious Georgetown University.

Of course, college in a city is not cheap. Tuition is often higher, while room, board, and living expenses are definitely pricier. The average student at AU pays about $33,000 a year, even after financial aid is factored in. Kyle Anderson, a senior at AU, told me that if he had gone to the University of North Carolina, a higher-ranked public school in his state, he would have paid about two-thirds less a year.

"I grew up in Greensboro, so Chapel Hill was an hour from my home," he said. "I had lived there my whole life. I was interested in politics but people didn't talk about it every day. I just wanted to go somewhere new and Washington, D.C., is the center of politics."

Since arriving in Washington, Kyle has completed four

internships, most of them during the academic year. Not only was the competition for those intern spots less intense during the school year (Washington is awash with interns during the summer), but the experiences also helped him better prepare for the demands of the workplace, because he learned to juggle a job and take classes at the same time. In other words, Kyle did exactly what employers said they want more of in today's graduates: he approached college as a mash-up of different activities to build his critical-thinking skills. And living in the middle of the nation's capital easily afforded Kyle a plethora of opportunities to do so.

Placing a Bet on a Location

AMONG THE FIRST UNIVERSITIES IN THE MODERN ERA TO leverage their urban location were New York University and George Washington University. In the 1970s and 1980s, both were seen as "commuter schools" that largely drew local students. At one time more than 50 percent of NYU's freshmen came from New York City. Today, less than 15 percent do. At the same time, George Washington University doubled its number of freshmen from New York, California, and Massachusetts. Both NYU and GW focused on building majors that connected them to what their cities were well known for—drama and film at NYU and public health and media at GW.

When Stephen Trachtenberg started as GW's president in 1988, he noticed that the university often talked about its urban campus but didn't involve students much in their surroundings. "The curriculum was so plain vanilla that it could have been offered at any university in America," he said.

Over the next two decades, through new buildings, programs, and marketing, Trachtenberg transformed the university into a national brand, one tied closely to its location in the center of political power. He recruited popular political journalists to teach media courses and invited CNN on campus to tape its nightly political show *Crossfire* with a live audience. "Our tag line was that 'something happens here,'" Trachtenberg said. "The implication was that nothing happens on other campuses."

Other urban universities followed the same playbook. In Los Angeles, the University of Southern California was trying to overcome its reputation as a party school in a bad neighborhood, which was partly a result of the 1992 race riots that played out on television screens across the country. After the riots, parents didn't want to send their daughters to South Central Los Angeles, and the number of women in the incoming freshman class dropped to 40 percent. Rather than run away from its location, USC unleashed a marketing campaign that played up its advantages, complete with photographs that set campus landmarks against a backdrop of skyscrapers.

USC's efforts paid off, moving "the university geographically in the minds of people, without a moving van," said Morton Schapiro, a former dean at USC and current president of Northwestern University. Like NYU and GW, USC also created and expanded majors that complemented the L.A. economy, in particular its communications program. Walter Annenberg, the late founder of *TV Guide,* donated more than $200 million to USC for its communications school, convinced that Los Angeles, and not New York City, had become the media capital of the world.

Annenberg definitely underestimated the enduring legacy of New York City as a media capital, but he was probably right to think about a university's proximity to an industry hub when placing such a large bet. And so should you. If you're sure of your major or future career, look for the cities where professionals in that field live. Start your college search around those places or be sure to intern in them.

When LinkedIn analyzed the skills that its members in the United States listed in their profiles in 2014, the online professional networking site found that workers in specific industries clustered around certain cities. Petroleum engineers were much more likely to be found in Texas, Louisiana, Oklahoma, and North Dakota. Manufacturing engineers were prevalent in Indiana, Ohio, and Pennsylvania, where automobile companies remain strong players. And those with skills related to the entertainment industry clustered around Los Angeles and Nashville.

So if you want to major in film, you probably should set off for a school near Los Angeles or New York City. Computer science? Probably San Francisco or San Jose. And music? Likely Nashville, New York City, or Los Angeles.

You can use LinkedIn to assist in your own college search. Its "University Finder" tool allows students to enter their major and the region of the country where they want to attend college to view popular campuses and employers for that particular career field. Enter "history" and "San Francisco," for example, and the tool suggests the University of California at Berkeley (Google is the top employer of its history graduates), San Francisco State (Kaiser Permanente is the top employer), and the University of California at Los Angeles (the top employer is the Los Angeles School District).

The rise of urban universities is similar to a story playing out in the housing market, where cities are enjoying a comeback among two enormous generations: millennials entering the job market and baby boomers downsizing from their suburban homes. As with real estate, the change in higher education is largely one of mind-set. Going to college fifty years ago meant traveling to a campus a short car ride away. In the 1960s, Ohio governor James Rhodes promised a college within thirty miles of every resident.

But since then, advances in technology that allow a video call on a smartphone, as well as easy and cheap transportation on discount airlines, have changed our concept of distance. New York students don't think that going to school in California is much of a stretch. So the best students have started to migrate to higher education institutions that are in or near a handful of cities—Boston, New York City, Atlanta, and San Francisco—that have a high proportion of college graduates.

"Choices are driven far less by distance and far more by a college's resources and student body," wrote Caroline Hoxby, a professor of economics at Stanford University, in a paper published by the National Bureau of Economic Research in 2009. With the best students clustering in cities, Hoxby found that half of the colleges and universities in the United States have become *less selective* in their admissions decisions over the past fifty years.

The Young and the Mobile

OVER THE PAST FOUR DECADES, AS MORE JOBS DEMANDED college diplomas, graduates started to move to places where those jobs were plentiful, and the nation became segregated along education lines. In 1970, nearly all major metropolitan areas had roughly the same percentage of residents with college degrees. But that balance no longer exists. Graduates have gathered in certain cities. The colleges in those cities have benefited greatly from this population shift, attracting students interested in jobs in the local economy who end up staying after graduation.

The image of the American "college town" has been redefined from the bucolic New England village with tree-shaded quads and ivy-covered neo-Gothic buildings to vibrant cities of "eds and meds." Today, in *every one* of the twenty largest U.S. cities, a college, university, or medical institution is among the top ten private employers in town. At least half of those top employers in five cities—Washington, Philadelphia, San Diego, Memphis, and San Jose—are eds and meds.

Indeed, one of the greatest influences on where college graduates settle after graduation is how many of their new neighbors also have a college degree. "College graduates want to be with other college graduates but in a diverse place, ethnically and culturally," Rosalind Greenstein told me. She is the research director at the American Institute for Economic Research. The Massachusetts-based institute publishes two annual rankings that don't get nearly as much attention as the *U.S. News & World Report* college rankings, yet are probably much more useful to students in the college search.

The first is the College Destinations Index, which examines some 270 metro areas across the country that have more than 10,000 students and ranks the top seventy-five areas based on four categories with the most impact on a student's off-campus college experience: student life (cost of living and ease of transportation), economic health (unemployment rate and entrepreneurial activity), culture (workers in innovative fields and entertainment venues), and employment opportunities (median earnings and research and development activity). The cities are separated into four groups based on population and then ranked. In the most recent survey, Boston; San Jose; Boulder, Colorado; and Ithaca, New York, came out on top.

The institute's second ranking explores where young people go to live and work after graduation. Much like the college rankings, the Employment Destinations Index looks at 260 metro areas and ranks the top seventy-five areas based on eight factors in two main categories that motivate job seekers to move: economic (how many people are looking for jobs and earnings for young grads) and quality of life (ability to get around without a car and number of bars and restaurants). The cities that landed at the top of this index were Washington, D.C.; Bridgeport, Connecticut; Ann Arbor, Michigan; and Iowa City, Iowa.

What should interest students most about these two surveys are the crossover cities that ranked high on both lists. Those are the places you want to consider for college, because they have a vibrant economy that can provide the opportunities you need outside of the classroom as well as full-time jobs after graduation.

The overlap between the two lists includes some of the usual suspects, such as Washington, D.C., and San Francisco, and smaller cities like Austin, Texas, and Raleigh, North Carolina. But it also includes places you probably didn't think had a strong job market in addition to being a great college town: Fort Collins, Colorado; Gainesville, Florida; Ann Arbor; and State College, Pennsylvania.

College Towns and Employment Hubs

These are towns and cities that were ranked high by the American Institute for Economic Research for the outside-the-classroom opportunities they provide to students while in college *and* as top destinations for young people to live and work after graduation.

Major Metro Areas

1. Boston	4. New York	7. Minneapolis-St. Paul
2. Washington, DC	5. Baltimore	8. Denver
3. San Francisco	6. Seattle	9. Chicago

Midsized Metro Areas

1. San Jose, CA	3. Raleigh, NC	5. Columbus, OH
2. Austin, TX	4. Pittsburgh, PA	6. Hartford, CT

Small Metro Areas

1. Ann Arbor, MI	5. Trenton, NJ	9. Omaha, NE
2. Fort Collins, CO	6. Huntsville, AL	10. Syracuse, NY
3. Gainesville, FL	7. Albany, NY	11. Honolulu, HI
4. Lincoln, NE	8. Anchorage, AK	

Smallest Towns

1. Ithaca, NY	4. Champaign-Urbana, IL	7 Lafayette, IN
2. Iowa City, IA	5. Columbia, MO	8. Bloomington, IN
3. State College, PA	6. College Station, TX	9. Morgantown, WV

Source: Author's analysis of the American Institute for Economic Research's 2015 Employment Destinations Index and 2014–2015 College Destinations Index.

Twentysomethings tend to be restless right after graduation. About a million recent college graduates cross state lines each year. Where they end up, as we saw in Chapter 1, is critical to how they spend the rest of their twenties and provides a peek into the cities that will likely power the country's economic engine in the future. As young graduates settle, everything else tends to follow, including big employers, start-ups, and new amenities.

"There is a very strong track record of places that attract talent becoming places of long-term success," said Edward Glaeser, the Harvard economist. "The most successful economic development policy is to attract and retain smart people and then get out of their way."

Every generation of college graduates has its hot city.

When I graduated from college in the mid-1990s, many of my classmates moved to Atlanta. Now Denver is the new place to be (its population of the young and educated is up 47 percent since 2000). Indeed, recent college graduates are often migrating west. According to a LinkedIn analysis of its members' online profiles, after earning their bachelor's degree from universities on the East Coast, nearly three times as many people moved to take jobs in San Francisco than West Coast graduates moved to New York City.

Some cities are natural talent magnets for new college graduates. The LinkedIn analysis found that new graduates were willing to move the farthest for jobs in San Francisco, Los Angeles, Seattle, and Phoenix. Meanwhile, other cities in the LinkedIn study—Boston, Pittsburgh, Philadelphia, and Baltimore—were able to better retain students after graduation because of the nearby industries that attracted them there in the first place. Those cities also tend to have a high concentration of colleges.

But these cities—and by extension their urban universities—may be challenged by an increasingly online world. The question for students is whether the rise of online learning, allowing them to take classes any time, anywhere in the world, will mean a college's location won't matter as much to them in the future.

Finding a Physical Place in a Virtual World

IN THE LATE 1990S, AS THE WORLD WIDE WEB EXPLODED into a global phenomenon, the popular sentiment on Wall Street was that online commerce would replace the physical world in the decade ahead. New companies sprouted up almost overnight that allowed us to buy goods and services—everything from groceries to videos to pet supplies—from the comfort of our own homes. Company valuations sky-rocketed, as everyone seemed to think that big-box stores and mom-and-pop shops were going to be wiped out by the virtual world. Of course, that didn't happen at the scale that was predicted, and the dot-com bubble burst in 2001.

Some online retailers survived the downturn. The biggest was Amazon. When Jeff Bezos founded the company in 1994, many thought he should have started by selling clothing. After all, consumers already bought clothes through mail-order catalogs. But Bezos reasoned that there was still a physical aspect to selling clothes, a "touch and feel" that was difficult to convey online. So he started with books, not exactly a hot seller at the time: they were the twenty-fifth most popular product category sold through catalogs. But as David Bell noted in *Location Is (Still) Everything,* about selling and shopping in the digital era, books were a perfect fit for the Internet.

"There is nothing about a book that you really need to touch and feel," Bell wrote. "If you know the price, the author, what it's about, and perhaps a bit of information from reviews, then you're good to go."

Fast-forward to 2001. Apple Computer was in the midst of a comeback, thanks mostly to iTunes and the iPod. But rather than beef up its existing online presence as Amazon did, Apple did exactly the opposite: it built a physical store and then a chain of them. Apple Stores offered a customer experience unlike that of other electronic chains such as Best Buy. It used the stores to curate its products rather than have the usual aisles and aisles of boxes. And Apple lent a cachet to its brand name by carefully selecting a limited number of retail locations, rather than opening in every market the way Target or Walmart does.

As with brick-and-mortar retailers in the late 1990s, a decade later colleges and universities faced similar predictions about the imminent demise of their vast residential campuses. The number of students enrolled in at least one online course skyrocketed from 1.6 million in 2002 to more than 6 million ten years later. But hundreds of colleges did not go out of business as was predicted (indeed, even Sweet Briar was saved a few months after it announced it would close). Online enrollments flattened. Surveys showed eighteen-year-olds had little interest in earning an entire degree online.

But many families cannot afford the cost of going to a physical college campus. In 2001, the average college tuition bill accounted for less than a quarter of an American family's paycheck. By 2013, it ate up more than 40 percent of median earnings in the United States. Most families will probably pay nearly anything for a Harvard degree, but many more are questioning whether it's worth it to pay Harvard-like prices at Podunk U., one state away. The irony, of course, is that wealthy schools like Harvard are able to give out significant financial aid to those who need it because they sit on top of hefty endowments, while needy students must take out massive loans in order to attend much less selective schools.

In the future, as the pathways through college become more varied, with some students arriving after a gap year abroad or transferring from community colleges, the very nature of a student's relationship to the residential campus and the physical location of a school will change as well.

Colleges will likely take a cue from the Apple Store and present the best experiences they can offer on physical campuses and then move the rest online. In other words, college will become a blended experience for many students, in that it will be neither fully in person nor all online. In this new world, location will matter even more than it does today, as internships, research projects, and other types of experiential learning for students will be nearly impossible to replicate online.

This blended strategy is exactly what brick-and-mortar retailers have followed in recent years, adopting what's called an "omni-channel" approach for consumers who shop in a mix of retail stores, online, and on their mobile phones. Such an approach allows retailers to focus on what's most important in their physical locations.

Author David Bell, who is also a professor at the University of Pennsylvania's Wharton School, believes that much the same thing could happen in higher education. He can imagine a future university where the best content is presented online, and then students go to a physical campus for the immersive experiences.

A tech entrepreneur in San Francisco is doing almost exactly that, having raised $95 million to fund his bold plan for a new university to compete with the likes of Harvard and Stanford.

An Elite, Residential, and Online University

"SAN FRANCISCO IS THE MOST SIGNIFICANT CITY IN THE world with a population under a million," Ben Nelson said, practically shouting at me over the din of city traffic nine floors below.

It was a mild February day in San Francisco, and we were standing on a long, narrow balcony of an office building overlooking Civic Center Plaza. Nelson was pointing out the surrounding landmarks as if he were the mayor of the city. To our left were the San Francisco Public Library and the Asian Art Museum. Just past them were city hall, the opera and symphony, and the San Francisco War Memorial and Performing Arts Center. Straight ahead, the University of California's Hastings College of the Law.

Nelson was showing what he considered to be the campus of the Minerva Project, that new university with $95 million in backing from venture capitalists. And its physical plant? I was standing in half of it—one rented floor in a nondescript, squat building on Market Street. Then Nelson pointed to the other half, a "dorm" in the far distance.

Nelson founded the Minerva Project in 2012 to remake how a college education is delivered in the United States and to rethink the whole idea of a physical campus. His goal is both audacious and unprecedented in the history of higher education: to build a name-brand, elite, liberal arts–focused university that costs about $28,000 a year in total, about half of what Ivy League institutions charge.

The key to Minerva's business model is its stripped-down

version of the prestigious modern American university. There is no campus with buildings designed by famous architects, no palatial recreational facilities, no expensive athletics teams. No classrooms, for that matter. All classes are virtual. The students take classes online even though they live together in the same city—in an apartment building in San Francisco's Nob Hill neighborhood.

Each year the students will move around the world, living in Buenos Aires, Berlin, perhaps Istanbul and Mumbai, among other cities. Students take their classes in the morning, freeing up their afternoons for internships and exploring the city, a perfect match of theory and practice, all while building resilience as they learn to navigate their way around real cities.

Unlike elite colleges that have put a lid on undergraduate enrollment even as demand for admissions has skyrocketed, Minerva's plan is to accept everyone who qualifies. "It's like if Apple and Samsung only produced enough phones to meet 5 percent of global demand," Nelson told me, pointing out that many colleges and universities reject students who easily qualify for admission.

Within the next decade, Minerva wants to enroll 2,500 students a year, some 10,000 students overall. (By comparison, Cornell, the largest Ivy League institution, enrolls about 14,000 undergraduates.)

Elite colleges are not increasing class sizes even as they receive record numbers of applications. Harvard's classes are no larger than they were twenty years ago. Out of the most elite colleges in the United States, only one has any substantial plan to increase its number of students, and that's Yale University. Though it's building a $600 million mini-campus in New Haven for additional students, it will welcome only eight hundred of them.

Like many entrepreneurs, Nelson's big idea is rooted in his autobiography. As an undergraduate in the mid-1990s at Penn, he spent much of his time on a lobbying effort to reshape how students were taught to think, an idea he first outlined in a research paper his freshman year. He wanted Penn professors to better integrate the university's unique location into their courses. His ideas were never adopted, and he graduated frustrated and disappointed with his Ivy League degree. "I realized I didn't get a good education," he said.

A few years after he left Penn, Nelson joined a start-up photo-sharing site called Snapfish, eventually becoming its president. When Snapfish was acquired by Hewlett-Packard in 2005 for a reported $300 million, he dusted off that freshman-year plan to remake undergraduate education and hired one of the world's foremost psychologists and a former Harvard dean, Stephen Kosslyn, to help him make it happen.

The success of Minerva's new model will rest on its curriculum and its technology. Every freshman takes the same four cornerstone courses: formal analysis (mathematics), empirical analysis (science), complex systems (social science), and multimodal communications (writing and public speaking).

"If you master those four systems of thinking," Nelson said, "then you can apply them to anything." These are precisely the skills employers say they are looking for in today's college graduates.

I told Nelson I still didn't understand why students all living in the same city should take their classes online. Most online universities have been created to appeal mainly to place-bound, time-pressed adults. Minerva was going after the opposite: the best students who have time to learn and the ability to go anywhere.

Nelson took me into an office to watch a class. As the session of "Multimodal Communications" began, images of students popped up across the top of the screen. Classes take place in real time and have no more than nineteen students, the size of a seminar at most colleges—except that a college seminar typically has an air of intimacy to it. This one felt oddly distant, even though the students, most of them in their apartments, were only a mile away.

Still, the discussions in the eighty-minute class were fast-paced. The students had to be ready to be called on by the professor at any moment. They couldn't be checking Facebook on another screen. Everything in the class was recorded, so students and professors could mark moments they wanted to review later on.

Minerva's first students enrolled in the fall of 2014. A few weeks into the semester, the students took a field trip to visit nearby Stanford University. The eight-thousand-acre Palo Alto campus is perhaps the best example of a university that has leveraged its place on the map to help its students launch their careers. It's right in the middle of tech-centric Silicon Valley, a stone's throw away from some of the biggest and most recognized technology companies in the world, many started by Stanford faculty and students: Google, eBay, Netflix, Yahoo!, Hewlett-Packard, LinkedIn, and Pandora.

As the Minerva students roamed the Stanford campus of low, red-clay-tiled buildings, a few officials at the start-up university casually wondered aloud whether some of their new students would want to return after exploring a physical campus where many of them could probably have gone. But after a few hours, they all boarded a bus back to San Francisco to get ready for their next online class. A year later, when Stanford welcomes a new freshman class to Palo Alto for the 130th time, this group of Minerva students will have moved on to their next city, Buenos Aires.

Established universities, of course, can't pick up and move each year like Minerva. Most of the nation's colleges were built for a different era, when being spread out geographically was seen as an asset, because it offered easy access for students wherever they lived. Today, with the ease of travel and communication, having a college in your backyard doesn't matter as much as being located in a dynamic place with an array of opportunities for hands-on learning.

If you're sure of what you want to do in life, look for the cities where professionals who have the skills you want to acquire already live and then either go to college there or intern there. As Minerva is trying to show, in the twenty-first century you can learn almost anywhere, but you can't apply that learning everywhere.

CHAPTER 5

HANDS-ON LEARNING
FOR A CAREER

Tell me and I forget; teach me and I may remember; involve me and I will learn.
—XUNZI, CONFUCIAN PHILOSOPHER

V ERY FEW OF US ENJOY SITTING IN A CLASSROOM LISTENING TO A TEACHER DRONE ON FOR HOURS ON END. WE LIKE TO LEARN BY DOING. WHEN WE were children, our parents didn't teach us to use a fork by showing a PowerPoint lecture. Our learning was hands-on, literally. Then we started school, and for the next decade and a half, we were mostly confined to seats in a classroom.

Such rote learning frustrated Herman Schneider. In 1885, he graduated from Lehigh University in Bethlehem, Pennsylvania, and set up an engineering practice in town. He hired graduates from his alma mater and other technical schools to serve the burgeoning local steel industry. Many of the new recruits didn't pan out. Though book smart, they weren't able to apply what they learned in school to the job. This problem fascinated Schneider, and a few years later when he was offered a teaching job at Lehigh, he jumped at the chance to try out an idea: students would work in local industrial plants to earn money for tuition *and* as part of their formal instruction.

But administrators at Lehigh found Schneider's proposal unworkable. To them, jobs in the local factories were manual and dirty, whereas a university's mission is to educate students in the life of the mind. So Schneider left Lehigh and moved to Pittsburgh, where the industrialist Andrew Carnegie had recently started the Carnegie Technical Schools (later renamed Carnegie Mellon University).

Carnegie had already spent some $13 million to build industrial shops on campus where students could practice their craft. An improvement, but this was not the real work environment Schneider had imagined, so he packed up again, this time for the University of Cincinnati, where he was offered a position as an engineering instructor. Eventually, he persuaded his colleagues that the bachelor's degree should include serious work experience.

The year was 1906, and the program marked the birth of what would become known as co-op education in the United States. Schneider's persistence helped usher in the modern era of learning by doing. In the decades that followed, experiential learning would spread throughout the American education system, although never to the extent and scale it did in European countries, such as Germany and Switzerland.

Indeed, U.S. colleges and universities today continue to have a strong bias against combining education with relevant work experience. The two approaches have long competed for attention on college campuses. There is nothing wrong with going to college to learn for learning's sake, but you need to resist the pull of schools that want you to focus your undergraduate years solely on the pursuits of the mind if you want to find a good job after graduation. The best college education is a two-prong approach that exercises both the mind and the hands.

That hands-on approach comes in many forms, from internships and co-ops to apprenticeships and, more recently, makerspaces, and we'll examine how they all are critical to the success of young adults today in this chapter.

The Evolution of Internships into a Corporate Recruiting Tool

THE PRACTICAL EDUCATIONAL EXPERIENCE MOST OF US are familiar with is the internship. It was first established after World War I by medical schools as a period of additional training for doctors after they obtained their degree but before they earned a license. In the 1960s, occupations outside of medicine began using internships, but they didn't really spread widely until the 1980s.

By 1994, when I interned at *U.S. News & World Report* in Washington after my junior year of college, internships had become a rite of passage on the way to a bachelor's degree. Each day I hopped on the subway with other interns I lived with that summer who headed off to prestigious-sounding addresses, from congressional offices on Capitol Hill to the Smithsonian Institution.

But unlike students of today, we didn't see our internships as another box to check in our journey through college or an extended tryout for a full-time job down the road. We had applied for our internships a few months earlier, and we were happy to spend the summer in Washington with a job that didn't involve showing up in a uniform or flipping burgers for minimum wage. Sure, the internships provided a much-needed line on what were fairly blank résumés to that point, but few of us really knew what we wanted to do with our lives, and those summer positions were not crucial to landing a job after college.

Over the course of the next decade the rules about hiring changed, as the war for talent began to move at alarming speed. These days, perhaps nothing illustrates the massive shift in how college graduates launch a career as much as the role the internship now plays—an experience taken for granted twenty years ago.

On an early November night, the Inn at Penn, a hotel on the edge of the University of Pennsylvania's campus in west Philadelphia, was buzzing with activity. Although a few employers were still interviewing seniors for full-time jobs, several firms were now focused on hiring interns—for the *next* summer.

The main event was a presentation by Goldman Sachs, the Wall Street investment bank. About 150 students streamed into a large ballroom on the second floor, most of them clad in dark suits with Under Armour and North Face backpacks slung over their shoulders.

Placed on each chair across the room was a one-page description of Goldman's intern recruiting events with the deadlines to apply and the dates for interviews. It was already too late if you wanted a technology internship; most of the other interviews would come in January. Goldman Sachs holds events like this on about sixteen university campuses nationwide, sending a clear but unstated message that if you don't go to one of those schools, you probably won't intern at Goldman Sachs.

Lauren Goldberg, a recruiter from Goldman Sachs, jumped up onstage to welcome the group. Since very few gathered here had a chance of getting an offer (about 59,000 students apply for 2,900 intern positions each year), her good cheer was helpful. She talked about the various players in the recruiting process, from university relation managers (that's her) to campus ambassadors to school team captains. She encouraged students to come to as many recruiting events as possible to network.

"Try to connect with as many people as you can," Goldberg said. "But don't e-mail too much."

She invited former interns to the stage to give advice. Differentiate yourself, the former interns said. Find something interesting that sets you apart. Make an impression. And if you run into a roadblock, Penn alumni are always willing to help. When Goldberg encouraged those attending to download the company's recruiting app called "Make an Impact," nearly everyone around me immediately pulled out their smartphones. I downloaded it, too. The welcome screen popped up: "This app is designed to prepare you for the recruiting process. This is your impact dashboard."

All of this—just for a summer internship.

After forty-five minutes, the presentation ended. A small group of students huddled around a table at the back of the ballroom, snacking on leftover food. As I talked with them, I discovered they were sophomores who had come to gather intelligence and get a head start for *next* year. One named Victor told me he had transferred from the University of Chicago because it was "too academic." Penn, he said, was known for "getting a good job." Victor and his friends were barely a quarter of the way through their college years, yet they were already trying to figure out how to jump through the next hoop. They knew as sophomores that a good job after graduation largely depended on first getting the right internships in college.

Internships are now a critical cog in the recruiting wheel for Fortune 500 companies and many smaller firms, too. Today, employers hire as full-time workers around 50 percent of the interns who worked for them before they graduated, according to the Collegiate Employment Research Institute at Michigan State University; at large companies (more than ten thousand employees) and in some industries (construction, consulting, accounting, and scientific services) the share of interns who get full-time offers is growing every year and is closer to 75 percent at several of them.

No one wants to be *the first* full-time employer anymore of new college graduates who haven't worked or interned anywhere.

As a result, the race to lock up the best interns early in their undergraduate career for full-time employment later is commonplace among employers of all sizes and in all industries. And that means that finding a summer internship as a college student is not like looking for a summer job in high school. In other words, don't expect to land a great internship if you wait until a few weeks before the end of the school year. The peak recruitment time for internships is February and March.

This new emphasis on the internship has upended the traditional recruiting calendar on campuses nationwide, and not only at the elite universities. With more companies hiring from their intern pools, recruiters have shifted their attention from hiring soon-to-graduate seniors as full-timers to scoping out juniors—even as early as the fall term to be interns the next summer.

"There was a time when 50 employers came to recruit for interns," Patricia Rose, director of Penn's career center, told me. "Now we have 180. They want to wrap up talent before anyone else."

Nowhere is that more evident than in California's Silicon Valley. Each summer, thousands of college students descend on the technology mecca to work as interns at a mix of start-ups and Fortune 100 companies. During those three months, these companies are looking for the best students in their intern pools—as well as those at other firms—and putting a full-court press on them to commit to permanent jobs after they graduate.

On almost any given day, in places from San Francisco to San Jose, companies host intern events that range from simple networking discussions to lavish parties. Facebook sponsors the most popular one of the summer—a carnival just for interns. Such perks, once reserved for second-year law- and business-school internships, have now filtered down to undergraduates in fields where there is a shortage of talent.

Before Adam Ward headed up recruiting at Pinterest, he worked at Facebook. That's where he first noticed that companies were hiring more of their interns for full-time jobs. Facebook had scoured data on its employees' performance and reached the surprising conclusion that how well they did on the job had nothing to do with where they went to college. The common trait among the company's best performers? They had all interned at Facebook. That led the social-networking giant to start hiring more of its own interns, and now the company turns more than half of each year's intern class into full-time employees.

Ward has a similar goal at Pinterest, where about one-third of interns are hired in permanent jobs. "It's a really smart way to recruit," he told me. "It's all about trying before you buy."

When LinkedIn analyzed the online profiles of its 300 million members to determine which fields were more likely than others to hire their former interns into full-time jobs, it found wide discrepancies between occupations. Nearly 60 percent of accounting interns were hired for full-time jobs at the same company within a year of their internship, while only 25 percent did the same in apparel and fashion.

Internships are increasingly the *only* way for new applicants to get in the door at some companies. Postings for internships now make up a significant proportion of the overall entry-level job openings in several industries, including engineering, graphic design, communications, marketing, and information technology.

"You can't spend your first couple of summers in college lifeguarding or working as a camp counselor anymore if you have a specific job in mind after graduation," said Matthew Sigelman, the CEO of Burning Glass Technologies, the company that provides real-time labor market data and has studied internship postings. "Those typical summer jobs are not going to position you for work after graduation."

Traditionally the summer intern fetched coffee and made photocopies, but not anymore. In many companies, interns perform real work, and employers are expecting interns to come with specific skills already in hand. Students with technology internships are expected to know programming languages like SQL and Java; design interns need to be proficient in Photoshop and InDesign; and every intern basically needs to know how to manipulate a spreadsheet in Excel.

"A job posting is flagging a set of expectations, and they tell us that even internships are asking for really technical skills," Sigelman told me. "It puts a lot of pressure on students to learn on their own outside their core academic program."

Early on in college, you must find internships and secure as many as you can before you graduate. This factor should be taken into consideration when deciding on a college's location, because you want the flexibility to add internships during the calendar year.

Equally important is the sequence of your internships. Each internship experience needs to build on the previous one. The first summer of college is a good time to test out a field before officially settling on a major the following year.

The internship after the sophomore year should be more fo-cused on what you might want to do after graduation and position you for the final internship before your senior year. With so many employers hiring from their intern pools, the last internship before graduation is perhaps the most important.

"He who gets them last gets them for good," said Adam Ward of Pinterest. In other words, if your heart is set on working at Google, then you should intern there within a year before graduating.

Wageless Work: Are Unpaid Internships Worth the Cost?

AN INTERNSHIP CAN DO MORE THAN JUST HELP YOU GET that first job; there is evidence it can lead to a lifetime of success. A 2014 Gallup survey of more than thirty thousand college graduates found that those who had had an intern-ship or job that allowed them to apply what they were learn-ing were *twice* as likely to be engaged in their life and work.

The problem was that only one in three graduates said they had internships or similar hands-on learning experi-ences in college. While internships have shifted from a nice-to-have line on a résumé to a critical component, colleges and universities rarely view them that way. Few schools re-quire internships as part of any formal degree program or provide much help to students in securing them, beyond posting a list of openings on a website or in the career center. Students I interviewed said they found internships by networking with classmates or by participating in on-campus clubs and activities. If you want to snag the best internships, you must investigate opportunities early on, much like the sophomores I met at Penn.

Choosing the right internships may be *the* most important decision you make in college. As Lauren Rivera chronicled in her 2015 book, *Pedigree: How Elite Students Get Elite Jobs,* internships at name-brand organizations are as critical as admission to a selective college. An elite internship "was a signal that candidates had successfully navigated a rigorous screening process and thus likely had strong cognitive and social skills," Rivera wrote.

In some majors, the internship experiences count more than the degree. That's what Laura Fiedelman discovered when she switched majors from art and history to public relations in her second year at the University of Texas at Austin. "No one cares how many degrees you have in PR," Laura said. "So I tried to get as much intern experience as I could."

Despite her late start, Laura had three internships by the time she graduated, each experience building on the previous one. Taken together, they gave her a good taste of the kinds of jobs she might find after graduation.

But even with those internships, Laura still left college without a full-time job. That's when she made a critical decision for her future. Rather than go back home to her parents in Houston, she moved to New Orleans for an unpaid internship at a boutique public relations firm. To support herself, she worked part-time at a fast-food restaurant.

"You have to want it so much," she said about pursuing a profession rather than just any job after college. "I worked thirty hours at the PR agency when they asked us to work twenty. And then I went to roll pitas for another thirty hours. A deadline of Friday meant Wednesday for me. I always underpromised and overdelivered."

A few months later, she was able to parlay that internship into a paid full-time job offer. But many of Laura's classmates weren't as fortunate. "One of my closest friends had student loans so she needed to get a job," she told me. "Now she's working the front desk at a hospital."

Laura had an advantage over many of her classmates: she didn't have any student loans. She could afford to take another unpaid internship after she graduated, whereas the 60 percent of undergraduates who leave college with debt cannot.

Unfortunately for students saddled with debt, the number of unpaid internships has increased dramatically in recent years, as industries look for free labor in a lackluster economy. Colleges have been complicit in the growth of this wageless work because employers of unpaid interns usually require them to receive academic credit before they can be hired. So not only aren't these interns being paid, but they must pay colleges thousands of dollars to guarantee they get academic credit.

While many students feel they must take unpaid internships to bolster their résumés, not all free experiences pay off like they did for Laura. Indeed, according to surveys by the National Association of Colleges and Employers and Intern Bridge Inc., *unpaid* internships rarely give students much of a boost in the job market. Seniors who have had a paid internship are about twice as likely to have a job offer at graduation as those who took an unpaid internship. Even more surprising is that the number of students who had an unpaid internship and *do* get a job offer is about the same as those *who never interned at all* in college.

So why did Laura succeed as an unpaid intern? She did her research about the internship and discovered two key things about it. She was sure she wouldn't be performing just menial work, and she confirmed that interns who had worked there before were quickly hired into paying jobs. Both of these played into the most important aspect of an internship: whether it will pay off in the form of a real job someday.

Too many recent college graduates take internships—they should really be called temp jobs—that never end with job offers or only lead to more internships. The risk in taking too many internships after college is that you end up becoming a perpetual intern, what some call a "permatern," and never find the on-ramp to a career.

Co-op Programs: Transferring Knowledge Between Learning and Work

WHEN HERMAN SCHNEIDER STARTED THE FIRST CO-OP program at the University of Cincinnati, twenty-six students signed up. The following year, eight hundred students applied. Within a few years, Northeastern University in Boston copied the idea. Schneider thought he had started a revolution in American higher education.

Yet more than a century later his idea remains a novelty, confined to a handful of campuses including Cincinnati and Northeastern, as well as Drexel University and Georgia Tech. The same opposition Schneider faced in the early 1900s still exists today: faculty members believe a college's job is to broadly educate students, and they remain deeply suspicious of anything that hints at vocational training.

Although they are often conflated in the minds of students and parents, co-ops are not internships. While internships are an add-on to a degree, co-ops are part and parcel of the undergraduate experience, making up anywhere from one-third to almost half of the time a student spends in school. They are paid positions and, as a result, often require more substantive work since students are dedicated full-time to a job and not splitting it with course work. They are much more intensive experiences that mix classroom instruction with on-the-job training.

Because co-ops more closely resemble an actual job than an internship does, they are good opportunities for students unsure of their major or who want to test out their career options.

When Jason Wong started his freshman year at Northeastern University, he was set on going to medical school. But within months, he started questioning whether a biology major was right for him. His adviser suggested that after his freshman year he apply to a co-op that would provide him a mix of experiences to help him decide about his major.

Jason landed a co-op at Massachusetts Eye and Ear Infirmary. For six months, he didn't take classes or pay tuition, all while he earned thirteen dollars an hour. In the morning, he tested newborns' ears, and he spent afternoons processing patient referrals, both serious jobs for a college sophomore.

After only a few weeks, "I definitely decided that I did not want to treat patients," Jason told me.

He switched his major to health sciences. At most schools, Jason might not have figured out that he had picked the wrong major until much later. His second co-op was at the Boston Medical Center, training clinicians on a new computer system. When the co-op ended, the hospital asked him to stay on, and for the next year, he juggled full-time work while he finished his courses at Northeastern. A month after he graduated, while many of his high school friends who went elsewhere to college were still looking for jobs or taking gigs as bartenders and waiters, Jason received a promotion.

Northeastern runs one of the country's most successful co-op programs. Over four years, students complete at least two paid co-ops that last from four to six months (or three co-ops if they complete a five-year bachelor's degree). The largest co-op program in the world is at University of Waterloo in Ontario, Canada, where almost half of its thirty thousand students alternate between four-month periods on campus and in the workplace.

Waterloo is a university you may not have heard of, but it kept coming up over and over again in my interviews with Silicon Valley CEOs and venture capitalists as a source of some of their best employees and ideas for start-up companies. Indeed, the president of Y Combinator, one of the most influential backers of new tech companies, traces the roots of eight successful start-ups to Waterloo.

Because of co-ops, Waterloo students are accustomed to toggling between long stretches in the classroom and the work world, while also being able to refine and reflect on what they learned in both places. This back-and-forth movement between theory and application trains the brains of students differently from how a traditional curriculum largely restricted to classroom learning does. It's also similar to the method most successful companies follow these days to develop new products. They test an idea with customers, make small changes based on that feedback, and repeat the process until they perfect it, rather than spending months or years huddled behind closed doors building something nobody wants.

One Facebook recruiter who likes engineering students from Waterloo told me they come better prepared because the theories explained in the college classroom have already been reinforced during their co-op jobs.

"Too many engineers are well versed in theory but have never been expected to apply what they learn to a real problem," the recruiter said. What's more, Waterloo graduates already possess the work habits and sense of responsibility often lacking in some of today's graduates who never worked before or during college.

Co-ops take advantage of how we learn best—in small chunks. The co-op schedule segments the learning of an undergraduate career into a series of sprints that, when added together, can equal the distance of a degree rather than expecting students to run one long marathon straight through for four years.

But work experience *alone,* whether it's through a co-op or an internship, is not what makes the graduate stand out when he or she is on the job market. The most successful graduates I found in researching this book were those who could translate what they learned in one context (the classroom, for instance) to another that is far different from where they originally learned the concept (a project at work). Educators call this "transfer learning"—the ability to generalize core principles and apply them in many different places.

The concept sounds simple enough, but today's students, facing the constant pressure to prepare for standardized tests, rarely have the chance to learn through problem solving or to be involved in the kind of projects that reinforce skills that can be used in multiple settings. Our ability to drive almost any car on the market without reading its manual is an example of knowledge transfer, as is our ability to solve math equations involving any number once we learn the basic formula.

Knowledge transfer is what gets you hired, because it's the ability to show in job interviews what you cannot easily display on your résumé or in an application.

Susan Ambrose illustrated the importance of transfer learning for me by telling a story about her arrival at Northeastern in 2013. Ambrose is senior vice provost for undergraduate education and experiential learning at the university. She was unpacking her office when she decided to take a walk around campus. She saw a tour of prospective students and parents and joined in. A parent asked about the co-op experience, and the student tour guide told them about his job where he learned to use Microsoft Excel while working on various projects.

Ambrose was perplexed by the answer and told the guide, "Excel is a tool to accomplish something, not what you actually learned."

"No, I learned Excel," the student replied.

"You were trying to understand patterns in the data, right? You were trying to create different scenarios to model for the future, right?" Ambrose kept quizzing him. "You were looking for trends, right?"

"Yes, Excel," the student answered again, somewhat confused by Ambrose's line of questioning.

Sure, Ambrose told me later, the student had acquired a valuable skill, but what he failed to understand was how to translate those underlying competencies—in his case creating a spreadsheet—to a range of activities he would someday be asked to do in another job.

"Transfer is one of the hardest things that human beings do," Ambrose said.

College students find the concept particularly difficult to grasp because for most of their schooling, their learning was directed by someone else, parents and teachers, who spelled out exactly how to transfer knowledge between disparate ideas. Learning in the workplace, however, is mostly self-directed.

Ambrose went on to interview more than one hundred Northeastern students as part of a study to learn about the co-op experience. What she heard in those interviews confirmed what she had surmised after her campus tour: students could describe what they did in the co-op, but they couldn't isolate what they learned from the job and how they could use that knowledge in the future in other settings.

As a result, Northeastern added courses before and after the co-op to help students figure out how to apply what they learned in the workplace to another context. Teaching students how to transfer their knowledge had a side benefit on campus. It helped faculty see the co-op experience as more a part of the academic fabric of the institution, rather than as a job alone.

"Co-op contributes hugely to the intellectual development of students," Joseph Aoun, Northeastern's president,
told me. "The emphasis has always been on professional development, but there are things that happen in the co-op
that are just not possible to teach in a classroom."

Since his arrival at Northeastern in 2006, Aoun has expanded the university's co-op network worldwide to 120
countries with 3,000 employers. I met Aoun at a White
House gathering of educators and entrepreneurs in the
summer of 2015, where he outlined the benefits of hands-on
education in today's volatile economy.

In his view, the dual training that is a hallmark of co-op
education is the best way to develop the soft skills so prized
by employers these days. Co-op education helps students
recognize the connective tissue between ideas and develop
tolerance for ambiguity in their work, which so many recruiters told me today's college graduates don't possess.

The focus of that White House meeting was preparing
students for an economy where the jobs of today could be
replaced by robots tomorrow. I asked Aoun if higher education was training students for jobs that might be obsolete in
a decade. He shook his head. Even the best artificial intelligence systems can't replicate knowledge transfer, he said.
While humans as young as toddlers can master a task, such
as learning how to play a video game, and then transfer some
of that knowledge to a similar game, computers have to be
programmed to learn each game from scratch.

For American education to remain relevant to students, it
must abandon the antiquated idea that schools and colleges
broadly educate people for life while employers train them for
jobs. It's not either-or anymore. Given the amount of money

parents and students spend on a degree, there is no reason colleges shouldn't provide both a broad education as well as the specific training and skills needed for the workplace. And one idea for marrying the practical arts with the liberal arts is gaining prominence after largely falling out of favor in the United States over the last half century: the apprenticeship.

The Rise of Twenty-First-Century Apprenticeships

THE JUNIOR YEAR OF HIGH SCHOOL IS PIVOTAL FOR STU-dents planning for college. It's the year they first take the SAT. It's the year they whittle down their list of colleges to visit over spring and summer breaks. And it's the year to shore up flagging grades on their transcripts.

In 2006, Michael Shinn entered his junior year at South Iredell High School, north of Charlotte, North Carolina. He had good grades, especially in math, and he had already completed several AP courses. As with generations of smart kids before him, Michael's teachers and guidance counselors pushed college as the only pathway to a solid future. Michael was firmly on the college track, with plans to major in mechanical engineering at North Carolina State University.

But like an increasing number of students, he was also anxious about paying for college. His family didn't have much money, and his parents had recently divorced. One day in the spring of his junior year, he noticed a sign in the guidance office for an apprenticeship program run by a group of local manufacturing companies.

Michael went to the presentation the next week. What he heard surprised him. The companies were nothing like the blue-collar, assembly-line plants his generation associates with factory work. These were advanced operations with a desperate need for workers who could actually think, workers who would not just make widgets. The best part was they would pay him to work and go to school, and they guaranteed a job after the four-year apprenticeship. He signed up.

Michael spent that summer on a tryout with Ameritech Die & Mold, which makes custom tools for plastic parts found mostly in automobiles. At the end of the summer, the company invited him to stay on, and he worked there part-time while finishing his senior year of high school. He then applied and was accepted to North Carolina State, but when the time came to make a decision, the apprenticeship seemed to be the better path for him.

"Going to college would require debt," said Michael, who was earning eight dollars an hour as an apprentice. "College was a lot more uncertain. I could graduate without a job. Not everyone can be an engineer."

Three years later he completed the apprenticeship and received an associate's degree at a nearby community college, all paid for by Ameritech, and he started work with a $35,000 salary. Today, at age twenty-five, he's married, owns a home, and is a new father, all life markers difficult to achieve for his high school friends who went to college. Many of them are struggling to find jobs in their fields or any good-paying job at all. Even his own wife, who recently earned her MBA, is finding the job market tough going.

"Teachers and guidance counselors only talk about college as the way to a good life," Michael told me. "College is not for everyone. I wish more of them could see what I do all day. I don't have a mindless manufacturing job."

Once again, the lack of knowledge that adolescents and young adults have about the wide variety of occupations that exist and what people actually do in those jobs hampers their ability to consider more than one pathway after high school.

In 1988, a commission convened by a national foundation published a landmark study about the American education system called *The Forgotten Half: Non-College Youth in America.* As the title suggested, the report zeroed in on the large proportion of American kids who skipped college altogether and argued that they were at risk in the future unless we paid greater attention to them. It recommended, among other things, enhanced training opportunities for students who did not go to college.

Like many reports of its kind, this one was released with much fanfare but then drifted away to bookshelves to collect dust. Over the next two and a half decades, the college-for-all movement took off. The primary solution proposed to help the forgotten half was to be sure they got a college degree. Despite attempts to improve access to college, the forgotten half still exists. Today, only 52 percent of young people have either a two- or four-year degree or an industry certificate by the time they reach their midtwenties.

The goal of universal college has actually done more harm than good, because it diverted attention away from any real discussion of alternatives to a college education, and it has banished anything that smacks of job training to second-class status. A lot of parents proudly boast when their sons and daughters are accepted to college but may be embarrassed if their children skip college for an apprenticeship.

As late as the 1950s, fueled by robust training opportunities in a variety of fields, there were many paths to a career outside of college. Like many of his generation, my uncle had a lucrative career as a bricklayer after completing an apprenticeship in the late 1940s. But apprenticeships disappeared over time, as the manufacturers and construction unions that largely sponsored them declined, and vo-tech education came to be regarded as outdated and a distraction from the college track. Today, less than 5 percent of American youth train as apprentices, mostly in construction.

Even the program Michael Shinn completed in North Carolina takes only a handful of students out of the hundreds who apply each year. Contrast that with European countries where apprenticeships evolved with the new economy in emerging fields from advanced manufacturing to banking. Perhaps as important is that parents and educators in Europe see apprenticeships as a highly respected pathway to a career.

Germany is often held up as the best example of how the apprenticeship system could work in the twenty-first-century knowledge economy because 60 percent of its youth are enrolled in training programs. But Switzerland probably provides better lessons for the United States.

"Switzerland is much less regulated, and its apprenticeships are in more diverse fields than Germany, where it's mostly manufacturing," said Robert Schwartz, codirector of the Pathways to Prosperity Network, an effort by a network of twelve states to ease the transition of young people into adulthood.

As part of that project, Schwartz has toured Swiss schools, training facilities, and companies to study its apprenticeship system. He told me he came away impressed by the

Swiss system and convinced that it could be replicated in the United States. "We have behaved as if college is *the* destination without addressing why," Schwartz said.

In Switzerland, compulsory education, which ends after ninth grade, is designed to give students the core academic skills. At that point, they can choose an academic path or a vocational path. The academic path is much narrower than the one in the United States and is focused on the few professions, such as medicine, where a university education is required. Only about a quarter of Swiss students choose the academic track. The vocational path is much more popular, with nearly 70 percent of students choosing it, and includes some two dozen areas of specialization from banking and retail to health care.

Beginning in the tenth grade, students rotate among three places for their apprenticeships—employers, industry organizations for training, and school—over the course of three to four years. The apprenticeship track immediately puts them into a work setting where they are mentored and coached, the learning is hands on, and they are paid (anywhere from $800 to $1,000 a month). They finish with a certification that leads to a job, because the curriculum is set by industry standards, not what professors want to teach or think students should learn. As a result, Switzerland has a youth unemployment rate that is the lowest in Europe and about half that of the United States.

There is evidence that American attitudes about apprenticeships are slowly changing. First, the number of apprenticeships is rising for the first time since the 2008 recession. Second, with college debt surpassing the trillion-dollar mark, students and parents are giving apprenticeships a second look as an alternative to paying sky-high tuition for a bachelor's degree that might not lead to a job. Third, some apprenticeships are beginning to have an academic component that makes them nearly indistinguishable from traditional colleges and usually leads to a degree entirely paid for by the graduate's ultimate employer.

"Apprenticeship is the other college, except without the debt," said Thomas Perez, the U.S. secretary of labor, who has the goal of doubling the number of apprenticeships to some six hundred thousand by 2018. He also said, "This notion that you either go to college or you get an apprenticeship . . . is just false."

The modern version of what an apprenticeship could look like for American students interested in alternatives to college is on display at the Apprentice School in Newport News, Virginia. The school, which serves the nearby navy shipyard, is housed in a new, state-of-the-art building that includes a gymnasium for its sports teams, computer labs, and classrooms. Students who choose from one of more than twenty occupational areas are paid an annual salary of $54,000 by the final year of the program—$10,000 above that of the average bachelor's degree recipient—and afterward they are guaranteed a job with the military contractor that operates Newport News Shipbuilding.

The school is just as selective as Harvard. It receives more than 4,000 applications each year for 230 spots, and significant numbers of its graduates go on to earn bachelor's or master's degrees. In many ways, it looks and feels like a typical American college, except in one important respect: its students graduate debt free.

Apprenticeships, along with co-ops and internships, often

require students to make deliberate choices about their career pathways, to seek out training opportunities in the corporate world or schools with co-op programs, or in the most extreme cases to get off the college track altogether. But not all hands-on learning needs to be so prepackaged and prescribed for students already overly scheduled and unsure about what they really want to do in life. Indeed, on a growing number of campuses, spaces are opening up for students to experiment, to tinker with their creative urges, and to practice their practical skills.

More than one hundred years after Herman Schneider fled Bethlehem, Pennsylvania, when Lehigh University refused to adopt his idea for co-op education, the university opened the ultimate hands-on training experience for students to pursue their ambitions.

The Makerspace: A Place for Self-Directed Learning

SOUTH MOUNTAIN IN BETHLEHEM RUNS ALONG THE southeastern tip of the Lehigh Valley. For generations, the thick-forested mountain of hardwoods overlooked the bustling factories of Bethlehem Steel on the valley floor below.

In the early 1960s, Bethlehem Steel opened three buildings the size of airplane hangars on a ridge near the top of the mountain. Inside, nearly a thousand engineers and scientists conducted research and development for the second-largest steel producer in the world. But within three decades, the American steel industry collapsed and the cavernous buildings turned into artifacts of the valley's famed industrial past.

Now Lehigh University is bringing the dormant buildings back to life as a giant industrial playground for a new generation of inventors and entrepreneurs. Think of them as much bigger versions of the Silicon Valley "garage," where some of the most iconic technology companies of the twentieth century were born.

At Lehigh, it's called "Mountaintop," and it not only looks completely different from the historic and shaded main Lehigh campus two miles away, but the industrial-looking campus is also designed to teach students how to think for themselves in an environment that stresses teamwork and hands-on learning.

Students earn a spot in the former Bethlehem Steel buildings by pitching research projects. They then spend their summers working on the projects in an environment that mimics many of their careers after graduation. They set their own schedules and let their curiosity shape the projects with little involvement from professors.

"There is an unleashing of student talent," Alan Snyder, a vice president at Lehigh, told me. "We let them play, we let them explore, and they find a thrill in the ambiguity."

As we walked through one of the complex's vast buildings, Snyder said the problem with a traditional college curriculum is it "waits too long to put people in over their heads." Mountaintop totally "shifts that perspective." The building we were in stretched the length of a football field, and the nearly two hundred students working on some forty projects were sprawled out in small groups on both sides of it.

One group of students worked on devices created on 3-D

printers to fit over the hands of stroke victims to help them move. A few yards away, another group had set up a series of child-sized plastic pools to study the breeding habits of endangered fish, while on the other side of the building students were attempting to design a better cinder-block hut for residents of Senegal. Because the students didn't come together through an assignment within a specific class, the groups were often made up of a collection of random majors.

The students working with endangered desert pupfish to determine how they could prevent other fish from eating their eggs even included some biology majors from the local community college. When the students were in charge of their own learning, they seemed less interested in what they needed to do to get an A and were willing to take more risks by following their ambition.

"We care about what we're doing because we designed it," said Emily, who was working with the group on prosthetic hands. "It's ours. No one is telling us what to do."

As I listened to the students' stories, they reminded me of young schoolkids on their first day of second grade, excited to tell others about what they had learned. Why couldn't learning be this engaging for students in college everywhere instead of the drudgery it often is? Why couldn't the academic calendar be as flexible as Lehigh's, so students could work and learn at a pace similar to what they will face in the workplace?

Dozens of colleges from Arizona State to the University of Nebraska at Lincoln to Case Western Reserve in Cleveland have opened up similar facilities in recent years, usually called "makerspaces" and modeled after the DIY maker movement. They all work in slightly different ways but usually have the same equipment—3-D printers, woodworking tools, and industrial cutters—and the same general goal: to bring together an eclectic mix of people from different academic backgrounds, from artisans and engineers to businesspeople, in the hope that the exchange of ideas and skills will create great inventions and products either individually or collectively.

Makerspaces have also opened in communities where they serve as a training ground for people who want to learn skills or need access to expensive industrial machines to start a business. Josh Mabry from Chapter 1 launched his business from ADX in Portland, where locals pay anywhere from $50 to $200 a month for classes and time using the equipment.

One of the problems with higher education today is that students are paying ever-higher tuition rates for the academic experience on campus when some of the most valuable learning opportunities increasingly happen outside the classroom or far from campus.

"It doesn't matter what you *take* in college, it matters what you *do*," Michael Roth, president of Wesleyan University, told me. "You should be able to show your teachers and then anyone else how what you've made in a class, what you created, demonstrates your capacity to do other things and what you're going to do next."

Hands-on learning is a critical component to your degree. No matter your major or whether you do an internship or a co-op or find other experiential learning opportunities in college, here are three competencies you want to walk away with from the experience:

1. Learn a Job

What college students know about possible jobs remains limited to the occupations featured in books or television shows or those careers familiar to them from their childhood. So when students sift through job openings as seniors, many titles sound as if written in a foreign language.

An internship or a co-op provides an opportunity to learn a specific job, but perhaps even more important, to witness what the people around you do for a living and get exposed to occupations you never knew existed. Worry less about the particular job you're doing—especially in those internships during your first and second year of college—and focus on learning new skills.

When I interned at the *Arizona Republic* the summer after I graduated from college, I wanted to cover breaking news but was instead assigned to cover technology for the business section. I filled in for a reporter who was on leave and ended up writing about a new emerging technology—the World Wide Web—which turned out to be one of the most important things I learned about in my internship.

2. Learn Social Skills

Majoring in one of the STEM fields might increase your chances of landing a job after graduation, but not if you don't also gain the soft skills laid out in Chapter 2.

Occupations that require strong social skills—cooperation, communicating clearly, and empathy—have grown much faster since the 1980s than technical jobs that are easy to automate, according to research by David Deming at Harvard University. Yet such social skills are rarely emphasized in schools or the formal curriculum in colleges. Look for internships and work experiences that will give you opportunities to work with others, rather than solely on individual projects, so you can learn to negotiate and showcase your teamwork skills to a potential employer.

3. Find a New Network

Although students increasingly are getting job offers from their internships, not all work experiences in college lead to full-time positions. Still, the people you meet during the few months of an internship can be helpful to your success after college because they tend to be what Adam Grant, a Wharton professor and author of *Give and Take,* refers to as weak ties. Such people travel in different circles from those of your closest friends or even alumni of your school, and thus they have access to new information. One study by sociologist Mark Granovetter found that you're 58 percent more likely to find a job by cultivating your weak ties rather than your strong ones.

If you don't gain those competencies during internships while in college, it's likely you'll end up searching for launch experiences—what I call finishing schools and postgraduate gap years—right after college to practice the job-related skills that should have come with your very expensive bachelor's degree.

CHAPTER 6

LEARNING TO LAUNCH

W HEN JACK BIRD WAS A HIGH SCHOOL SENIOR IN ASPEN, COLORADO, HE LISTENED TO ALL THE ADVICE ABOUT HOW TO GET A JOB RIGHT out of college. He had a strategy. He picked a practical major, engineering. He decided to go to college in the heart of the red-hot Silicon Valley job market. And he made a point not to take on too much debt to pay for his bachelor's degree.

But as with many plans forged at age eighteen, Jack's began to change after he arrived at Santa Clara University in San Jose, California. He was less interested in his engineering courses than he'd thought he would be, so he switched to environmental science and added political science as a second major. He earned mostly A's and B's and found a job as a research assistant on campus for extra cash and the requisite line on his résumé.

By almost every measure, Jack was shaping up to be a

Sprinter. In the spring of his junior year, he traveled to Zambia for a research fellowship focused on sustainable farming techniques. By the time he returned for his senior year in the fall of 2013, he wasn't that concerned about the job search on the horizon.

"I was thinking, 'How hard can it be to get a job?'" he recalled.

Jack, like so many of his generation, thought a job was the trophy waiting for him at the finish line of college. No one told him otherwise, not his professors or the university's career center. No one emphasized the importance of internships beginning the summer after his freshman year. Nor did they encourage him to start the job search early in his senior year. Most of all, he received little guidance about how to describe what he accomplished in college to prospective employers during interviews.

"I had all these awards. Good grades," he told me. "I wasn't thinking it was that urgent. I was holding out hope that I could stay in the Bay Area.

"It was, to say the least, a pretty idealistic picture," he admitted.

He decided to take another paid summer research fellowship after graduation, this time in Mexico. When he returned to California in the late summer, his college friends already had jobs. He started to look, and that's when he panicked.

"I quickly realized that I was going to be scrambling," he said. "Not only was I several months behind my classmates, but I was having a tough time trying to make ends meet."

His nearly $18,000 in student loan debt and a pricey apartment near school didn't seem like such great ideas anymore. Jack applied for every job opening he could find at environmental companies. When he didn't receive any responses, he widened his search and applied for any job anywhere and heard nothing back.

That's when a friend suggested he take a break and rethink his plan, so he wouldn't be forced to take a dead-end job. The friend mentioned a new program in Seattle called Koru that was helping recent college graduates land on their feet by providing them with tangible business skills and the one-on-one career coaching that's missing from undergraduate education.

That night Jack applied to Koru. He had an interview and was accepted the following week.

Finishing Schools for the Bachelor's Degree

KORU IS THE BRAINCHILD OF KRISTEN HAMILTON, A former Microsoft executive, and Josh Jarrett, who headed up the higher education innovation programs at the Bill & Melinda Gates Foundation. The pair understood from their previous roles just how broken the job market was for recent college graduates. On one side, employers complained that students were unprepared for the workplace; on the other, higher education officials accused companies of unloading their training responsibilities onto colleges. Students undertaking the first real job search of their young lives were caught in the middle.

Backed by $12 million in venture capital, Koru is designed to fill the gaps in students' résumés and bridge the divide between what employers want and what colleges actually teach. It puts students through an intensive three-and-a-half-week program that includes a rigorous real-world project commissioned by an employer in one of the three cities where the company has set up shop.

Think of Koru as a finishing school for undergraduates. It is part of a growing constellation of what I call post-college launch experiences that come at the very end of the senior year of college or right after graduation. Like gap years before college, these launch experiences better prepare students for their careers through a short spurt of crash courses, such as at Koru, or much longer multiyear fellowships, such as at Teach for America, which places recent graduates as teachers in struggling schools for two years. In some cases, these postgraduate programs have become de facto graduate schools and can provide key markers on résumés that help students jump further ahead in their careers faster than if they acquired a job straight after graduation.

With graduate school debt now accounting for 40 percent of the $1.19 trillion of outstanding student loans, these postgraduate experiences are gaining traction, even with colleges themselves, as a less expensive alternative to additional schooling. Noah Leavitt, an associate dean at Whitman College in Washington State, which offers Koru as an option for its students and alumni, told me such skills-based business courses aren't typically offered as part of a broad liberal arts curriculum. Before Whitman partnered with Koru, the college considered offering a similar program itself. But officials concluded that it would take years for the liberal arts college to build the expertise for the program and develop the relationships with employers that are a hallmark of the Koru program.

Although bridge programs like Koru have existed for a few decades, their numbers and enrollment have increased significantly since the 2008 recession, as students and their parents have become much more anxious about the post-college job market. The programs all work in slightly different ways, but in general they offer anywhere from three- to four-week crash courses in business fundamentals to recent college graduates who have little or no experience translating a balance sheet, developing a sales presentation, or designing a strategy. Some of these postgraduate programs are run by colleges themselves, while others are controlled by private companies.

Either way, the courses are not cheap, especially after students have paid out tens of thousands, or hundreds of thousands, for a bachelor's degree. The programs range in price from a few thousand dollars to more than $10,000 for the oldest of them, the Tuck Business Bridge at Dartmouth College's business school. Compared with Koru, which is focused mostly on teaching business skills through a group project, Tuck is fairly traditional, with students spending most of their four weeks in classrooms running through the basics of finance, economics, and marketing with MBA professors.

In recent years, because of demand and new competitors, Tuck added a three-week program over winter break. Middlebury College in Vermont offers a winter program as well, which delves into a more eclectic set of topics than the others, including crisis management and creativity, and is offered to Middlebury undergraduates as part of their tuition.

Candice Olson envisions such bridge programs as the "new passageway" from college to career, and not just an advantage for the privileged few who can afford it right now.

This new passageway would be a discrete time period in a young person's life that is separate from college and allows students to unlearn the bad work habits of their undergraduate years and gain the specific skills to be ready for a job on day one. Olson started a postgraduate launch program called Fullbridge in 2011, after she sold iVillage, an Internet company that focuses on women. Fullbridge offers students a mix of online classes taught by well-known professors on subjects such as workplace communication and time management, coupled with case studies and in-person coaching and role-playing sessions. Like the other bridge programs, it also includes a group project. Fullbridge offers its own four-week boot camp in Boston for around $5,000 and has joined with colleges to offer programs for their students, including Holy Cross, Tulane, and Miami Dade College.

Bridge programs seek to provide a direct pipeline to a job. Though a handful of colleges have recently beefed up their career services—some make the career center the first stop on tours for high schoolers—don't be fooled by the word "placement" that many offices still include in their titles. They don't really do anything close to helping place students in jobs.

Campus career offices provide generic help with writing cover letters and finding job listings. In contrast, the bridge programs market themselves essentially as a job service and can align their offerings to and partner with specific employers to give their students a foot in the door.

The Seven Competencies for Success
in Fast-Growing Companies

BEFORE HAMILTON AND JARRETT STARTED KORU IN 2013, they spent nearly a year meeting with fast-growing companies to find out what distinguished their best new hires from everyone else. "The rock stars were those who, over and over again, stepped up to solve problems," Hamilton said. "They were very focused on solving problems that seemed to be in front of them, without waiting to be assigned a project or told what to do next."

Hamilton and Jarrett found common threads in what they heard and used them to create the "Koru 7," the seven competencies they identified as most predictive of high performance: grit, rigor, impact, teamwork, curiosity, ownership, and polish (many of these are similar to the skills outlined by employers in Chapter 2).

"It's not that these skills are not learned in college; they are not taught," Jarrett said. "They are too often learned by osmosis, and we're focused on them explicitly."

Take a business presentation. When students do presentations for a college class, they are often graded on the content, not on how it's delivered. They also only do it once, so they never get a chance to apply feedback to improve their work.

Koru focuses on polishing the communication skills used in business presentations because, as Jarrett told me, it is the "skill easiest to improve [on] in a short amount of time." At Koru, students practice various business skills the way a musician attacks a new piece of music, with drills and lots of practice—followed by immediate, genuine feedback. It's a much different rhythm from that of a long college semester, where students grow accustomed to far-off deadlines. "New college graduates are not ready to turn around a research study in thirty-six hours," Hamilton said. Koru attempts to change those habits quickly.

Koru moves fast, dividing its three-and-a-half-week program into three parts. Students first come together in Seattle, San Francisco, or Boston to learn business skills not developed in college, such as interviewing customers, coming up with product ideas, and making presentations to executives. In the middle part of the program, students apply those skills through the "employer challenge," during which they help a company solve a problem on the tight deadlines frequently found in business environments. This is also where students get to spend time with an employer so both sides can figure out if there is a fit for a full-time job when the program ends. The final piece of the course includes one-on-one career coaching to help the students practice their interviewing skills and plan their next moves in the game of life. Throughout the program students have small-group discussions with hiring managers and short classes on business communication and networking.

After the four years it takes to earn a bachelor's degree, a four-week program seems too short to effectively learn everything you didn't in college and launch into the job market. But Jarrett said Koru's goal is to get students out of their comfort zone, and there is "only so much time students can hold that state before the learning diminishes."

Almost 85 percent of Koru students find jobs within six months of completing the program. It's unclear whether those college graduates would have landed jobs without Koru's help and whether the program's $2,700 price tag is worth it. After all, not everyone needs to learn the specific business process skills Koru focuses on, but some students and parents are willing to pay anything to get a leg up in a competitive job market.

Koru's employer network is really its top selling point because it serves as a matchmaking service for students and firms that are hiring. Many of the employers Koru works with are start-ups or fast-growing companies with huge talent needs—Wayfair in Boston, Yelp in San Francisco, and REI outside of Seattle. The program's graduates get jobs everywhere, but many of them end up at companies they were first exposed to through Koru.

Karen Jobe, a human resources manager at Zulily, an online clothing retailer, told me the company has partnered with several groups of Koru students on projects to help build its men's business and also to better attract expectant moms. Jobe said she has hired about a dozen Koru graduates as a result, and they stand out from other recent just-out-of-college hires for being able to learn from their failures. "Most college grads have gone through college and were told they're great, so they can't accept negative feedback on the job," Jobe said. "Koru grads at least come into the job knowing how to receive feedback and improve on that feedback."

Companies see Koru and other bridge programs as a source of already vetted and trained job applicants. Both qualities are key to employers in an era when a college degree alone provides a fuzzy signal for predicting professional success and when young workers rarely stay in jobs very long. The bridge programs allow companies to feel more confident in taking a chance on a broad set of job applicants. Top employers can already hire the best graduates from the most selective schools. But employers claim that it is difficult to find graduates from less selective schools who would be a good fit because there is more uncertainty about their skills and abilities.

Yet employers have remained unwilling to spend the time or money to add additional campuses to their recruiting schedule or to sift through stacks of applications to find that rare candidate from a random college. Instead, they take the easy way out and recruit mostly at selective schools because they know the admissions offices at those places already did the sifting for them four years earlier.

What's different now is that the talent pipeline has many more conduits flowing into it from around the world, in far-flung places that could yield great talent even though corporate recruiters will never visit them. That's why bridge programs have real potential to disrupt the traditional way corporate recruiting currently works on campuses.

We are already getting a glimpse of the future as a few colleges incorporate bridge programs into the undergraduate curriculum well before graduation, just as students are choosing their major and when they need help lining up critical internships. As the programs move deeper into the undergraduate pipeline, the next logical step is for bridge programs to act as scouts for graduates much like agents for Hollywood actors and professional athletes. Bridge programs offer the career guidance and coaching that students desperately want and need these days but are not getting from their undergraduate institutions.

A First for College Graduates: Negative Feedback

ON A RAW, EARLY JANUARY DAY, I ARRIVED AT KORU'S headquarters in Seattle's Lower Queen Anne neighborhood a few blocks from the city's famed Space Needle. The sixteen students in the Koru class were designing a social media campaign for a local company, Porch, that connects homeowners with contractors. Working in groups of four, the students developed surveys, fanned out into the city to interview potential customers, and studied competitors.

On this day, the students were practicing their presentations for a final pitch to executives that would take place the following week at Porch. Koru leaders evaluated everything from the language students used to how they dressed and their nonverbal cues. Jarrett peppered the groups with questions about the lack of specificity in their survey questions and how they analyzed the data. He was particularly tough on their storytelling skills. None of the groups' pitches was persuasive or focused. Jarrett told them to use more precise language so busy executives could follow along. At times, the Koru team's criticism was harsh, and from the students' reactions it was clear they had probably never received such negative feedback.

The afternoon was a short course about the basics of business communication. The students were accustomed to communicating by text, and writing an e-mail to someone they met at a networking event seemed like a foreign concept. In college, they had learned to write research papers and the proper style for footnotes, but little of that matters in the job search or on the job. The instructor showed examples of e-mails sent by previous Koru students. They were either too casual or too long, and many lacked a point or any specific request. These e-mails had been written by graduates of some of the country's best colleges and universities, but it was clear they were incapable of writing a simple message to someone they wanted to work for.

I wondered about all the unemployed college graduates who weren't here, who didn't want or couldn't afford to pay a few thousand dollars for Koru (after what they'd just spent on a bachelor's degree)—the graduates who had received diplomas on commencement day with a promise that the very expensive piece of paper was a ticket to a better life. Most colleges don't worry about what happens to their students once they cross the stage at graduation, except when it comes time to solicit them as alumni for a donation.

In 2015, the federal government mandated that for-profit colleges demonstrate that their graduates earned enough money to repay their loans or risk losing access to federal student aid. About 1,400 programs were under scrutiny as a result. Traditional nonprofit institutions, however, were largely exempt from the rules. Their role isn't to prepare students for a specific job like the so-called career colleges. Their mission is to give teenagers a broad education that is supposed to make them employable for life. That's their job even though at one out of every ten American four-year colleges, a majority of their undergraduates end up earning less than $25,000 a decade after enrolling.

Although the needs of students and employers have changed, colleges cling to their historical mission. Too many students today lack the necessary coping skills and grit to succeed, and they end up in workplaces unwilling to invest in training them. Even the companies considered best in their industries have reduced what they spend on employee training by some 15 percent since 2006. "The goalposts have moved," Jarrett said.

Yet colleges are still playing by the old rules on a field built for a previous century. They still regard their role in the transition from college to career the same as they always have—as an interested observer and passive coach. Career services on many college campuses are merely an add-on amenity to the bachelor's degree, "somewhere just below parking" as a matter of administrative priority, in the words of one university president.

This is why bridge programs are catching on, and why many colleges and universities need to play catch-up in how they are preparing students for a career.

The Pathway to Selected Careers

WHEN JACK BIRD ARRIVED AT KORU FOR HIS FIRST DAY OF training, he quickly noted a few differences from a typical day in college. For one, the time at Koru was much more intense. Students were expected to show up on time, and they often worked late into the night on their projects. Time spent on a task and the ability to focus on a rigorous project are what researchers have found defines success in the workplace better than grades or major do. Jack also told me the reviews of his work were among the toughest of his young life. Most of all, Jack said that Koru taught him how to better explain to potential employees what he did in college.

In the middle of his Koru course, Jack met with a recruiter for LinkedIn. Jack's group was working with the online networking company on its employer project, trying to figure out how to attract millennials to LinkedIn's content. "I knew I had the skills to work at LinkedIn," he said, "but if I had sent my résumé there, I would've been just a number," especially as a graduate from Santa Clara University.

New college graduates rarely get the chance to meet face-to-face with a company recruiter, and their résumés often end up in the rejection pile before they even have an opportunity to sell themselves. For Jack, the twenty-minute chat with the LinkedIn recruiter turned into an hour-long conversation about Jack's time in Africa and Mexico. Until then, Jack told me he hadn't been able to explain how what he'd learned in his overseas experiences might apply in another setting, such as a job at a tech company.

"Koru helped me articulate the skills I had obtained elsewhere," Jack said.

Mock interviews and sessions with coaches assisted him in making the connections between the classroom and the real world. Undergraduates gather experiences in college, but no one helps them organize what they learned into an articulate and compelling story. A few weeks later, Jack was offered a spot in a full-time training program at LinkedIn.

It was a paid position that most likely would lead to a permanent job.

Bridge programs are not for everyone, and they're certainly not the only springboard to a career after graduation. They serve certain types of employers with particular needs for talent, usually in sales, marketing, or business development. The programs may not prove as helpful to students who want to work for the government or in nonprofit organizations, where mission is more important than the bottom line.

Not all undergraduates are ready to jump right into the workforce a month or even three months after college, just as students are not always cut out for college immediately after high school graduation. You'll recall from Chapter 1 that being a Sprinter doesn't necessarily mean you start a job the day after college. Yet that's the next hoop most students aspire to jump through once commencement is over.

It's what the author William Deresiewicz calls "credentialism," where the goal in life is simply to collect gold stars. In his book *Excellent Sheep,* Deresiewicz bemoaned the fate of graduates of prestigious schools who immediately head off to careers in finance and consulting. Half of the graduates of Harvard and Penn go into one of those two industries and more than a third of those at Cornell, Stanford, and MIT.

Deresiewicz is not alone in criticizing both smart college graduates for thinking too narrowly about their careers and the schools they attend for encouraging such thinking. These students have the widest range of options, yet most of them take only a few select paths to a job in finance or consulting, or law or business school, and a few years later many despise what they are doing. After hearing from so many unhappy recent graduates, one disgruntled Ivy League–educated lawyer decided to do something about it, and in 2011, he created a new option for launching from college.

A Post-College Gap Year

HIS NAME IS ANDREW YANG, AND HE HAS CREATED WHAT is essentially a post-college gap year (or two years in this instance).

Yang graduated from Brown University in 1996 and, like so many accomplished students who went to elite colleges with thousands of other strivers, he wasn't sure what he wanted next, so he followed the herd to law school. After law school, and needing to pay off his loans, he took a job at a big law firm with a six-figure salary. He hated it. He left within a year to start his own tech company. When that failed a few months later, he landed a job at a software company, and by 2006, he was CEO of a test-prep company helping students study for the business-school entrance exam, the GMAT.

In the five years Yang led the company, he saw many people like him. In this case, they had followed a route to business school because they didn't know what else to do. They ended up with jobs as high-powered consultants or on Wall Street and made more money than they ever thought they would. But, like Yang in his law office, they weren't happy either. By then they were in their late twenties, with nowhere to turn without returning to school for a different degree.

But Yang knew there was a tremendous need for the type of talent that ended up unsatisfied in law firms and investments banks. The need was particularly acute in cities like Detroit, Baltimore, Cleveland, Cincinnati, and St. Louis that many might consider second-tier cities because they don't have the cachet to attract young college graduates. But those cities have a start-up culture that is just as strong as those in Silicon Valley, New York City, and Washington, D.C.

This is where Yang saw an opportunity. Like Koru, he wanted to be a "connecter," but in this case between upstart firms and talented recent graduates before they headed down what he saw as the wrong path to graduate school. He knew young companies were responsible for long-term job growth but that in recent years their numbers were declining. For the first time in the nation's history, a majority of U.S. workers were employed at firms with five-hundred-plus workers. Yang was familiar with the success of Teach for America, which in less than three decades had placed forty-two thousand recent college graduates as teachers in schools and had a rejection rate that rivaled that of Harvard.

What if there was a similar program for entrepreneurs? Yang essentially copied the playbook of Teach for America and even appropriated part of the name for his idea: Venture for America (VFA).

VFA is a nonprofit organization that partners with start-ups in cities such as Baltimore and Detroit and pairs them with recent college graduates. For two years, the new graduates work for the companies in industries that vary from e-commerce to clean technology. The students earn a salary of around $38,000 a year and at some companies can even earn equity in the start-up.

The 150 fellows accepted into the program each year, who fan out to one hundred companies in a dozen cities, all begin with a five-week bridge program, where they learn about product design, public speaking, and, of course, entrepreneurship. Many of the fellows told me that this is where they first found their tribe—students like themselves who wanted to carve their own independent career path instead of simply following everyone else into the jobs that already existed. According to Yang, "entrepreneurship is an isolating endeavor," especially on college campuses.

Only recently have schools started to embrace the idea of entrepreneurship by offering courses or even degrees. The University of Maryland's president has publicly said he wants all thirty-seven thousand of the university's students "exposed to the concepts of innovation and entrepreneurship." But at many colleges and universities, the idea of embedding entrepreneurship into the curriculum is rejected as a passing fad. "If you go to career services and say, 'I'm going to start a company,' they'll push you toward a job because they worry you'll show up in some statistic as unemployed," Yang told me.

VFA fellows also said they chose the program because they saw it as an insurance policy for their bachelor's degree in a constantly evolving job market. According to a survey conducted by the *Chronicle of Higher Education* and American Public Media's *Marketplace,* a quarter of employers say they place less value on a bachelor's degree in hiring today than they did five years ago. Some 43 percent said they weighed work experience over academics when it came to hiring recent graduates, and 70 percent said they would ignore the requirement of a college degree altogether if the other characteristics of the candidate were a good fit.

Conventional career advice these days is to get a diploma

in something that leads to a job. That's why high school counselors and parents push finance, coding, and STEM majors. But there are no assurances that today's hot jobs requiring a college degree will remain that way for the next ten or even the next five years. Technology is rapidly replacing jobs we once thought were safe from robots. You might recall that a decade ago, web design was a hot major. That work was soon replaced largely by technology (WordPress), and the field evolved into higher-level tasks. Now the skill to have is user-experience design, though there's no guarantee that will remain in demand either.

About half of VFA graduates remain in start-ups in some way after the program, either as founders of their own companies or by working for one. For the VFA fellows I met, entrepreneurship offered the flexibility that traditional careers lack, especially when entire career fields collapse. Entrepreneurs can work for themselves and reap the benefits of their hard work in start-up companies and, most important, can also pivot quickly using the skills they have learned when the economy suddenly shifts. As the head of university partnerships for IBM said in Chapter 2, he'd rather hire someone from a failed start-up than a new college graduate any day.

Go Off the Beaten Path

IN RECENT YEARS, THE MEDIA HAS DONE A LOT OF REporting about the decline of the once mighty Detroit. More than seventy thousand properties in the city were foreclosed on in just one four-year period. Blocks and blocks of homes were left without basic services, such as running water or working streetlights. Giant potholes lined the roads. Sixty years ago, Detroit was one of the richest cities in the country, but by the 1970s people were leaving in droves. You get why graduates would flock to Seattle to join up with Koru, but it makes no sense why they would go to Detroit.

Yet that's just where I found Tim Morris on an early November day. I arrived at the Guardian Building, where he works, after passing through a maze of streets filled with construction vehicles, tall cranes, and people. This was not the Detroit I had imagined after reading the *Time* magazine cover story about its bankruptcy with the ominous headline "Is Your City Next?"

It was bustling, even booming, with trendy restaurants and expensive loft apartments. Inside, the Guardian Building was a monument to Detroit's storied past. Originally the headquarters for the Union Trust Company in the late 1920s, the building's three-story vaulted ceilings have been meticulously restored. Tim, an architecture graduate from the University of Virginia, explained how the giant columns were formed by travertine marble imported from Italy, with the base of each one held up by black marble from Belgium. Tim grew up in Georgia and had never seen a building so elaborate. And he wouldn't have if not for the push VFA gave him after graduation.

"Detroit would have been the last city on my list to move to," he explained.

Like many other college students, Tim majored in a subject that intrigued him in high school, but one where he had little idea what a full-time job in the field would really entail. Before his senior year at UVA he interned at an architecture firm in Atlanta. That's when he first witnessed what daily life would look like after college.

"The guy next to me was designing bathrooms for handicap accessibility, when I was designing parks and museums in college classes," Tim said. "I wanted to do something with more impact."

When he returned to UVA for his senior year, he looked into jobs at a nonprofit or for the federal government in Washington, but he worried that a career in a bureaucracy would lead to long stretches of unsatisfying work. That's when he heard about VFA from a friend (again, I was reminded of how networking affects the way college students hear about internships and jobs). He read Andrew Yang's book, *Smart People Should Build Things,* and was inspired to join VFA.

"Washington, D.C., didn't need me," he said. "It had too many young, talented college graduates."

Tim took almost the opposite approach to location from the one I laid out in Chapter 4, because he found a specific growth opportunity in going to a city off the beaten path that still offered the benefits of an urban location. Instead of going to a place where college students were clustered, he went to Detroit, where there was less competition from other recent graduates and where he felt he could stand out. With the help of VFA, he was placed in a start-up that designs innovative workspaces.

"You can have an ordinary job in a location like this, and it could suddenly become extraordinary," he told me.

Tim has already helped design a sculpture for a new public park in the city and is helping work on a new data center for Quicken Loans, which is headquartered in downtown Detroit and led by Dan Gilbert, who has donated more than a million dollars to VFA. Tim is committed to VFA for two years and remains comfortable not knowing what will come next.

"I don't have a five-year plan," he said. "I want to see where this takes me next. So many people are focused on getting *a job* after graduation that they don't want to wait to see if anything else is waiting for them around the bend."

Tips for Launching from College

ALTHOUGH THE POST-COLLEGE LAUNCH PROGRAMS clearly help some graduates quickly find their way, not all recent graduates can afford to enroll in one or move to a new city for two years to work at a start-up. After all, many have student loans to pay off (about 40 percent of VFA fellows have student loans).

But any resourceful student should be able to replicate the set of valuable skills taught by programs like Koru and VFA while still in school by picking rigorous majors and courses and by finding rewarding part-time jobs, internships, and research projects. By observing the post-college programs, I found that they repeatedly drilled these four skills into their participants:

1. Find a Rhythm to Your Day

Many students now enter college without ever having held a part-time job in high school. The number of teenagers who have some sort of job while in school has dropped from nearly 40 percent in 1990 to just 20 percent today, an all-time low since the United States started keeping track in 1948. Some of that can be blamed on a lackluster youth job market, of course, but most teenagers are unemployed by choice. In upper-middle-class and wealthy neighborhoods, in particular, they are too busy doing other things—playing sports, studying, and following a full schedule of activities booked by their parents.

There is no replacement for managing a part-time job in something totally outside of your career field. Research has shown that students who are employed while in high school or college allocate their time more efficiently, learn about workplace norms and responsibilities, and are motivated to study harder in their classes so they can achieve a certain career goal.

A job teaches young people how to see a rhythm to the day, especially the types of routine work teenagers tend to get. It's where they learn how to show up on time, keep to a schedule, complete a list of tasks, and be accountable to a manager who might give them their first dose of negative feedback so they finally realize they're not as great as their teachers, parents, and college acceptance letters have led them to believe.

Working part-time while going to school also improves self-awareness. The employers I interviewed said that today's college graduates are willing to work hard to get the job done. But all of them had stories about the behaviors they found unacceptable: checking Facebook incessantly on their computers, leaving in the middle of a team project meeting to go for a workout at the gym, or asking for a do-over when an assignment went awry. A student who attended a Full-bridge program in Boston told me he was surprised when the sessions weren't canceled after an overnight snowstorm. He said professors in college regularly canceled classes for all sorts of reasons, including the weather.

Colleges increasingly treat students as customers, leaving them unprepared for the travails of full-time work. This is so at even the most elite colleges and universities, as *New York Times* columnist Frank Bruni discovered when he taught a course at Princeton: "From the moment I arrived on campus to the moment I left, I got the message that the students were my clients, and I was told more often about what I owed them, in terms of unambiguous explanations, in terms of support, than about what they owed me, their professor."

Post-college launch experiences can provide a healthy dose of reality in a short amount of time, but part-time jobs in school can give students the same sense of the pace of their next thirty-plus years of work.

2. See Models for How to Fail

FAIL FAST AND CHEAP reads a sign just inside the entrance of the Koru offices in Seattle. It's a mantra of start-up companies everywhere: stop when you fail and tweak your idea before you spend too much time or money. In Chapter 2, we heard that employers are looking for workers who have learned from their failures. But students rarely see good models of failure in their daily lives to emulate because parents and teachers often hide their mistakes. Instead, students are encouraged to follow successful examples. Even as students search for colleges, they are bombarded with marketing materials from institutions that showcase only successful alumni.

Students rarely see the trial and error that lead to good careers. They are only shown the final answer to a problem. Art Markman, a prominent author and psychology professor at the University of Texas at Austin, said he shares the "awful drafts" of his papers with students to show them that good writing doesn't just happen, but rather is the result of multiple iterations.

Where the bridge programs excel in particular is at helping students to accept failure through their projects because the feedback is not associated with a grade like in school, but is used to improve students' work over a short amount of time. Too many assignments and experiences in a young person's life are linked to a grade or a trophy rather than a genuine sense of accomplishment for a job well done.

3. Cultivate a Sense of Confidence

The era of the "helicopter parents" (who help their children do everything) and "snowplow parents" (who remove all barriers in front of their children) has caused students to enter college without the experience of doing things on their own. At the same time, colleges have added advisers and software programs that tell students which classes to take or majors to pick. So students graduate without the confidence in their own choices that they will need for the workplace, where they aren't provided with a list of *exactly* what to do to get a good performance review or a raise at the end of the year.

A student I met named Ham enrolled in Fullbridge as a college junior so he would be better prepared for his internships. He told me the bridge program opened his eyes to the gap between the accommodations professors were willing to make for him in college and the strict expectations of the workplace. And he went to Grinnell College, one of the best liberal arts institutions in the country. "Fullbridge gave me the push and confidence to take risks," he said. It allowed him to see what it was like to bask in the accomplishment of a job well done or suffer the consequences of his failures.

After the program ended, he returned to school to begin the search for a summer internship. Ham wanted to intern at Facebook, but he knew the odds were stacked against him given the number of applications the company received each year. Late one night in his dorm room, while working on an app he was developing, Ham decided to hunt around for the e-mail addresses of Facebook executives and found one for Sheryl Sandberg, the chief operating officer. He e-mailed her on a whim, describing his background and the app he was working on.

To his surprise, she responded and put him in touch with the head of global recruiting. He completed the online application, interviewed a few weeks later, and received an offer. Ham was a bolder, surer person because he was pushed to discover talents at Fullbridge that college hadn't previously teased out of him.

4. Seek Out a Mentor

A few years ago, I wrote an article for the *New York Times* about academic advising in college and sat in on several one-on-one sessions between students and advisers at Temple University. What struck me about the sessions were how focused they were on tactical issues—what classes to take, the requirements for a course, or how to switch majors—rather than advice on how to approach college.

When I was a reporter for the *Chronicle of Higher Education*, I often stopped in to see professors in their offices during campus visits and discovered they were happy to see me, because so few students ever came by for a chat. Undergraduates don't seek out professors or advisers nearly as much as they should to talk about life and careers. The same is true when students go on internships and are surrounded by professionals who could provide great advice for their careers.

Many of the Sprinters I met while researching this book talked about the substantive relationships they had developed with professors in college or mentors they sought out in their internships and first jobs. In Koru, students don't have a choice but to meet with career coaches in regular sessions. Such mentors don't necessarily have to be older or more experienced. The post-college experiences I observed in Seattle and Detroit had plenty of peer-to-peer learning, too.

Tim Morris told me he had an instant network of colleagues because of the other VFA fellows who were in Detroit. In most cities where graduates settle after college, they are forced to create such networks, which can help in everything from the job search to the apartment hunt. As you think about where to settle after college, consider how you might build your network of advisers or just sympathetic friends through work, community activities, or hobbies.

Finally, the post-college launch experiences help students tell their stories, giving them the ability—for perhaps the first time in their lives—to transfer what they learned from school to another context, the world of work. We'll dive deeper into storytelling in the last chapter.

The ability to create a narrative about what you have learned in school and in your jobs will become increasingly critical as the knowledge economy demands much more from workers and will require people to find learning opportunities throughout their lives. For generations, the traditional four-year degree was enough to succeed in just about any thirty-year career. But when everyone seems to have a bachelor's degree, the undergraduate experience is finally getting a desperately needed makeover to better prepare graduates for the lifelong learning that is now a fundamental part of any career.

CHAPTER 7

REDESIGNING THE BACHELOR'S DEGREE

The illiterate of the 21st century will not be those who cannot read and write, but those who cannot learn, unlearn, and relearn.

—ALVIN TOFFLER, AUTHOR AND FUTURIST

NEARLY 40 PERCENT OF AMERICAN WORKERS HOLD A BACHELOR'S DEGREE. COLLEGE GRADUATES ARE FOUND IN VIRTUALLY EVERY PROFESSION. Fifteen percent of mail carriers have a four-year credential, as do one in five clerical and sales workers and eighty-three thousand bartenders. Getting a bachelor's degree is what going to college means to most Americans and is so ingrained in our culture that students who don't march along are often admonished, questioned, and considered failures.

But the one-size-fits-all bachelor's degree was never de-signed to serve the millions of students of varying academic capabilities and professional interests it does each year, nor was it intended as the sole training mechanism for a job. In today's constantly shifting job market, where technology accelerates change in what employers demand, the bachelor's degree alone cannot provide all that young adults require in their formal training. Students and parents must recog-nize other legitimate pathways through education after high school, including community colleges, and educators need to establish new credentials that measure learning in a vari-ety of venues and are accepted by employers.

For now, though, the traditional bachelor's degree remains the dominant delivery system of American higher education. It's a credential rooted in the industrial revolution that spawned it, even though today's students process information and communicate in radically different ways. Colleges are reluctant to fiddle with the inner workings of the bachelor's degree, unsure what's in the magic box that leads to a success-ful graduate. The reality is that the modern four-year degree is what it is today simply because that's what colleges and universities have offered for centuries. Tradition seems to be one of the biggest obstacles to change.

What's the Magic of the Bachelor's Degree?

THINK OF THE BACHELOR'S DEGREE AS THE FOUNDATION of a house built in the middle of the seventeenth century. Over the following decades, courses and majors were built on top of that foundation, and they grew and evolved, as if you just kept adding more and more rooms to the house.

By the end of the twentieth century, a typical large university offered more than two thousand courses, even though most students take just forty courses to earn their degree. Smaller liberal arts colleges usually had a thousand courses listed, basically one for every two or three students enrolled there. Faculty members who saw themselves as keepers of the curriculum felt that they could teach anything they wanted as long as they could find a few students to fill a course.

At the same time, the number of academic majors grew by 20 percent between 2000 and 2010. More was added to the bachelor's degree, from internships to new course requirements for majors, as well as remedial classes for students who were not really prepared for college-level work—and all of it was crammed into the four-year window as the public demanded more students graduate on time.

The bachelor's degree was supposed to help you figure out what you wanted to do with the rest of your life and then land you the job that would start you off on that career trajectory. But in today's workplace, the bachelor's degree can no longer meet the differing expectations of both students and employers. Simply put, the bachelor's degree is overdesigned, with too many options and not enough focus or practical applications.

How did this happen? Why did colleges and universities keep expanding to a point where the bachelor's degree is now teetering on its foundation? To find out, we need to go back to the founding of the country.

The first colleges in the American colonies—Harvard, the College of William & Mary, and Yale—imported much of their structure from Europe: the four-year degree, the organization of the curriculum into courses with finite time blocks, even the titles "freshmen," "sophomores," "juniors," and "seniors."

Harvard actually started with a three-year degree but switched to a four-year plan by 1654, and most of higher education followed, of course. The undergraduate curriculum was relatively limited by today's standards. It consisted largely of courses derived from the classic liberal arts, which were seen as the best preparation for lawyers, ministers, and statesmen: grammar, rhetoric, logic, astronomy, arithmetic, geometry, and music. The college degree was certainly not the admission ticket to enter a profession as it is now. Most people entered careers through apprenticeships, where they studied with a master teacher and practiced new skills as they learned them.

After the American Revolution, however, colleges expanded their curriculum to respond to a growing nation. But as they added programs, colleges never culled any of the course work that already existed. Religion expanded to include philosophy. Then the social sciences, such as economics and sociology, were added.

In 1828, Yale released a widely cited report on the curriculum that said students should study a variety of topics to develop all areas of their mind. By the middle of the century, though, the president of Brown University worried that higher education institutions were going to become obsolete if they solely focused on exercising students' brains rather than also training them for jobs. He worried, in particular, about the need for civil engineers to build railroads.

Thus started the first debates over the purpose of college—should it provide a broad education or training for a job?—that continue to this day.

In 1862, in the midst of the Civil War, President Lincoln signed the Morrill Act, which gave land to the states to build agricultural colleges. Kansas was the first state to take advantage of the law and others followed, creating a national network of land-grant colleges that eventually became behemoths in their states—Michigan State, Penn State, Oregon State, and Iowa State. In addition to agriculture, programs were created in mechanics, engineering, and manufacturing. The number of vocational majors took off over the next century, as programs and entire schools within universities were created in education, business, public administration, and journalism.

No longer was the bachelor's degree the common experience it had been. The degree came to signify a random collection of 120 credits. Even within institutions, students arrived at their degree in vastly different ways, depending on their major. An engineering student might need 100 credits to complete a major, while a history major might need only half that. That fractionalization of the undergraduate experience led to a backlash in the first half of the 1900s and, as a result, many colleges and universities added a core curriculum that all students had to follow, usually in their first year.

As enrollments grew with the arrival of the baby boomers in the 1960s and 1970s, a required list of courses fell out of favor with students and faculty alike. They were replaced by

what were commonly referred to as "distribution requirements," meaning students had a choice of courses to take
within a broad area, such as the sciences or the humanities.

The bachelor's degree that emerged at the turn of this
century intensified the debate that had been simmering for
decades about the purpose of college. Today employers want
graduates pretrained for a job. That has resulted in a move
away from liberal arts majors on campuses—particularly the
humanities, which make up just 7 percent of new graduates in the United States—as students see college purely as a
means to an end, the job.

In an annual UCLA survey of first-year students, freshmen
now list getting a better job as the most important reason to
go to college. A decade ago, the top reason given was learning about things that interested them. Practical degrees are
in vogue. Business is the most popular undergraduate major
now and colleges have revamped their academic programs
to make them likely to lead to a job. At Lewis University
in Illinois, among others, for instance, you can even get a
bachelor's degree in social media.

With college seen as the only means to a job over the last
decade, enrollment surged. So too did the number of college
dropouts, because campuses often welcomed students who
didn't have the academic chops to finish a degree. Today,
only 33 percent of students at public universities get their
bachelor's degree within four years; 57 percent graduate
within six years. The numbers are not much better at expensive private colleges. Just over half of students graduate
in four years and 65 percent within six years.

Why do so many students struggle to graduate on time or
at all? Some of them arrive on campus with aspirations that

never match their talents. They want to be a nurse, but run into trouble with biology. Often they are like a customer looking at the wall of televisions at Best Buy, overwhelmed by the seemingly endless options, choosing trendy majors over ones more suitable to their personalities and skill sets.

For colleges, the solution to boosting graduation rates is to limit choices for students. Rather than using college as the time to explore subjects and careers they never knew existed, students are now assigned lanes based on their academic history. This channeling is largely achieved through technology. A handful of big public universities, including Georgia State, Virginia Commonwealth, and Arizona State (where I'm a professor of practice), have adopted computerized advising systems that track students' progress in classes and mine data on tens of thousands of grades to make suggestions on what courses should come next for them.

The advising systems all work in slightly different ways, but the theory behind them is the same one that drives the invisible array of algorithms that recommend music on Spotify and movies on Netflix. Colleges know that if you don't do well in statistics your freshman year you're not likely to finish a degree in economics. At universities with massive course catalogs to negotiate, the ultimate goal of these computerized advising systems is certainly admirable, even necessary. But they take away the ability of students to manage the ambiguity that will mark their daily lives in a few years. Students may make it to commencement, but they will more than likely struggle later when they work in an environment not designed by a bunch of algorithms.

Here's the fundamental problem: too many schools adhere to a historical model of the four-year degree that was designed for a much smaller and more well-prepared slice of students than the group they are serving today. Schools have tweaked their curriculum plenty of times over centuries to respond to the changing needs of the nation. But now the time has come to remake the bachelor's degree, too.

Three major universities—Georgetown, Arizona State, and the University of Southern California—are doing just that, and even students who don't go to one of those schools are beginning to carve their own pathways through college to ensure the bachelor's degree gives them the hands-on, practical knowledge they need to get a job.

Reimagining the Bachelor's Degree

ACROSS FROM WASHINGTON, D.C.,'S GEORGETOWN UNIversity is a red clapboard house where this 226-year-old Jesuit university is trying to reinvent itself.

Georgetown has long enjoyed a top twenty-five spot in the *U.S. News & World Report* rankings and a stellar reputation among prospective students, who often choose between it and the top Ivy League universities. But Georgetown's endowment of around $1.4 billion pales in comparison to that of the University of Pennsylvania ($10 billion), Princeton ($9 billion), or Stanford ($22 billion). Without that kind of financial cushion, Georgetown's biggest boosters worry it may not continue to attract top students in the future, especially with an annual price tag of more than $60,000.

The "red house," as it is known around campus, opened in 2014 as an incubator to rethink the university's future.

The cramped house is filled with posters dotted with sticky notes and elaborate drawings of models showing how students move through their undergraduate years. The chief architect of what happens in the house is Randy Bass, the vice provost of education and a popular figure on campus who still teaches undergraduates. Bass, who has a salt-and-pepper beard and a dry sense of humor, has focused much of his work in the last year on finding an avenue to increase the value of a Georgetown degree.

Bass told me higher education suffers from a measurement problem. "We only charge for a portion of what students see as the value of moving to a degree," he said. Tuition is tied to the credit hour, and 120 earns a bachelor's degree. But the credit hour doesn't actually measure how much students learn. It's simply an arbitrary measure of time spent in a seat, and it certainly doesn't tell employers much about the college graduates they're hiring except that they had the discipline to make it through four years of courses.

What's more, a degree based on time spent in a seat is inefficient because it forces all students to follow a single route to graduation (which, as we've seen, is not how the workplace operates). A new degree taking shape at Georgetown aims to strike out those inefficiencies and, at the same time, marry two competing interests: job skills and education. It would combine a liberal arts *bachelor's degree* with a vocational *master's degree,* all within the time frame of four years. Several universities already offer combined degrees, of course, but they typically take five years, and the master's experience is usually bolted on at the very end, almost as an afterthought.

Instead, Georgetown is rethinking the entire track to the degree. Professors have identified the competencies students need to learn for the merged undergraduate and graduate degrees. At most colleges, such competencies are tied to a course. Sit in a fifteen-week class and you've achieved the goal. By identifying the competencies associated with a degree, Georgetown can move away from the course as the sole measure of learning. Students could earn a competency in a fraction of a course or, more important, outside the walls of the university in internships or projects.

"That stuff that has been on the margins of the experience now are the bread and butter of this new degree," Bass said. "They are at the center of what we do."

The combined degree probably won't be less expensive than the four-year degree is now, but Bass believes it will be packed with more value. About one-third of Georgetown seniors already go part-time in their last semester because they have completed their degree requirements. In the future, perhaps they can get a master's degree during the downtime until graduation. Traditionalists keep asking Bass where in his model the bachelor's degree ends and the master's begins. But he envisions it as one integrated experience, where the undergraduate studies shrink over four years as the work associated with the master's grows. "Just maybe," Bass said, "we are creating a new kind of degree."

Such a degree is designed for the kind of student that Georgetown typically attracts—top of their class, academically focused, the type that usually sprints into a job after college. But college students are no longer the homogeneous group they were three or four decades ago. Yet they are still largely served by a one-size-fits-all delivery method—forty courses equals a bachelor's degree. Now, when technology allows much of the content of those classes to be delivered outside specified time periods each week and even anywhere in the world, the idea of "the course" seems antiquated and increasingly irrelevant to growing segments of today's students.

A few years ago, within one week on two different airplane flights, I was seated next to a recent college dropout. One left Ohio University after one semester, and the other dropped out of a performing arts college in Los Angeles after two years. Both had accumulated debt. Coincidentally, they both were looking to the cruise ship industry for work. They both told me the same thing about their short college experience: they weren't stimulated by introductory courses that lacked any connection to the real world. Indeed, the best classes in college often come in the last year, the "capstone courses," as they are called, where students have intimate learning experiences usually centered on hands-on projects. Students shouldn't have to wait four years for such engaging learning experiences.

An experiment at Arizona State University, a massive public institution with seventy-six thousand students, might eliminate the idea of a course altogether. Backed by a $4 million grant from the U.S. Department of Education, the university is testing out a degree in which students learn the subject matter for their majors through a series of projects instead of a specified schedule of classes. Engineering students might build a robot, for example, and they could learn the key principles of mechanics and electronics from faculty members as needed during the project. If students are struggling with a concept, professors could pull together an impromptu class or students could learn on their own using other resources, such as free online courses offered by other universities.

Unlike Georgetown, which is trying to prove its value among a select group of elite colleges, Arizona State's goal is to build new degree pathways that allow it to enroll a greater number of low-income students, a group that the nation's top colleges have mostly ignored.

The design of the project-based degree at Arizona State focuses on how students actually learn, said Betty Capaldi Phillips, the university's former provost. In a traditional course-based degree program, students might study a concept in the fourth week of a semester, but not use it until two semesters later, by which time they probably have forgotten what they learned. Or students have no idea how a theory is applied in the outside world as they are learning about it, so they quickly lose interest. By learning a new concept while working on a project, Phillips said, "you use it and you know why you use it."

Build Your Own Degree in the School of Life

EVERY YEAR, SOME FOUR HUNDRED THOUSAND AMERI-can students stray off the path to a college degree. Their reasons for dropping out are varied. Many struggle with academics and money, but a lot are frustrated with a bachelor's degree that seems disconnected from the job world, like my two seatmates. A few think they could carve a better path to a career themselves, outside the formal system. That was Weezie Yancey-Siegel. The San Francisco native dropped out of Pitzer College in 2011 in the middle of her sophomore year. She had traveled to Mexico for a class the previous summer, and while there, she started to doubt her motivation for going to college.

"I was learning a lot of things, but not the kinds of things I'd need to get a job out of school," she said. "After being in Mexico, I felt I could learn outside of school."

At first she intended to take off only a semester. But as she made plans for her time away from Pitzer, she found a lack of resources for students who wanted to design their own curriculum. So Weezie started a blog called *Eduventurist* to help students create alternative paths through higher education. Through that effort she discovered Enstitute, a two-year program in New York City that at the time had placed students in full-time apprenticeships and built a curriculum around their work on topics including finance, history, computer programming, and sociology. She applied and was accepted.

She spent two years in an apprenticeship with Sascha Lewis, one of the founders of Flavorpill, a digital media company in New York. In addition to working her way through Enstitute's semiformal curriculum, Weezie sampled free online classes offered by major universities, watched several iTunes U lectures, and learned computer coding by taking a few classes in New York.

"I know that I have learned a lot," she said, "and it's extremely frustrating to me that I didn't get credit for it."

She has ruled out returning to Pitzer but not to formal higher education some day. "A lot of my friends who went to college had trouble getting hired because they didn't have the experience. I have the experience piece, but I do worry that my dream job will require a degree," she said.

Weezie pieced together her own education, something most students can't do on their own. Many can barely navigate the system that's already laid out for them. But what if students picked colleges based not on majors or football teams or even their size, but on their buffet of options for earning a degree? In such a system, eighteen-year-olds could choose various educational routes after high school instead of just one. There would be multiple on-ramps, and once on these pathways, they could switch directions or exit at virtually any point.

This is what the bachelor's degree and a college education is going to look like for more students in the future. You can already take some of these different career on-ramps right now, as I outlined in previous chapters:

A gap year in which students collect valuable work experience while trying to figure out what problem they want to solve in life.

A combination work-education route where students toggle between a campus for a few weeks at a time and a real-world job.

An easy-on/easy-off lane so that students might exit after twelve months or twenty-four months to take a job and reenter a few years later when their skills need an upgrade before returning to the workforce.

And, of course, the traditional pathway that 20 percent of students today pursue by going directly to a residential four-year college and exiting four years later.

Whichever way students choose, one thing is certain: the college degree of the future will be more "modular" than today's; it will allow students to pick and choose how they reach the end point so they are no longer constrained by artificial limits on course hours, semesters, or years in school. Imagine this future degree as a Lego set. Most people build the picture on the outside of the box, just as most students today follow similar routes to a degree. But think of everything else you can build with the pieces inside a Lego box. Consider the possibilities for how one might piece together a degree that better fits the motivations for going to college and develops the skills needed in the workforce of tomorrow.

The most valuable of those degrees will provide a mix of academic disciplines interwoven with workplace experiences and hands-on projects. That is the idea behind the Jimmy Iovine and Andre Young Academy for Arts, Technology and the Business of Innovation at USC. It's a joint venture between the music producers Iovine and Young (better known as Dr. Dre), who launched the popular Beats headphones and sold the company to Apple for $3 billion. The goal of the program is to blend three disciplines that historically students wouldn't have been able to get in one place at the university: art and design, technology and engineering, and marketing and business.

In 2013, Iovine approached USC with a $70 million donation for the academy because he was worried that innovation was at risk in the nation's schools. To him, everyone was being squeezed through the same narrow pipeline to college and starting off with a steady diet of large, generic general education courses that stuffed their brains with abstract concepts and rewarded the accumulation of random facts. The worst students found college boring and eventually dropped out; even the best students found classrooms confining, as they lived in a creative world where they wanted to work on something.

"The kid who's going to have an advantage in the entertainment industry today is the kid who speaks both languages: technology and liberal arts," Iovine said. "That's what this school is about. The problem with the school system is that a lot of it's cookie-cutter, so what we're trying to do is disrupt it a bit."

Iovine hopes the program will spawn the next Steve Jobs, or at least fill a critical need for creative and tech-savvy leaders across industries. One afternoon in April near the end of the program's first year, I visited students who were part of the inaugural class. The program is housed in a large rotunda on the top floor of USC's student center, a space known as the Garage, which is filled with 3-D printers, hacksaws and laser cutters to fabricate products, and lots of whiteboards. Hardly any wall is straight, a reminder for everyone—both figuratively and literally—that students can't be boxed into classrooms or majors like elsewhere on campus.

The program's students hang out in the Garage at all hours of the day and night, eating meals as well as taking classes. In other words, they *want* to be in this kind of learning environment. Every few weeks they are divided into groups and given a challenge to solve. Their first challenge was to model what the music experience for listeners might look like a decade from now. After that the students worked on designing wearable medical devices and a skateboard plan for USC's campus. The program requires students spend much of their senior year setting up a business prototype, although most of these students have done that and more by the time they finish their first year.

USC's program, which mixes classroom learning with hands-on and creative projects, should be the norm in this new economy for students. Instead, the academy serves only two dozen of the three thousand freshmen who enrolled at USC last year. On the day I was there, some of the students in the program were huddled around a table debating the market for a product they built, an electronic overlay that enables blind people to use smartphones. "We're creating what's next instead of waiting for someone to give it to us," said Arjun Mehta.

In seventh grade, Arjun cofounded a company called PlaySpan that eventually turned into a product for digital payments and was sold to Visa for nearly $200 million. He then started another company that built an online learning platform for students and teachers. Arjun told me he seriously considered skipping college altogether until he found out about the USC academy (of course, he had that option as a multimillionaire). For Arjun, USC offered the best of both worlds—an informal and formal curriculum. He'd have the freedom to create his own path yet would also earn a much-needed college degree. Arjun's academic experience is a far cry from the 17 million undergraduates enrolled in higher education, "because I'm creating it myself."

The Underrated Value of a
Community College Degree

THE UNITED STATES IS LARGELY SEGREGATED ALONG EDU-cation lines. Those who went to college usually know mostly other people who did as well, and they tend to think their experience is universal.

Too often and for too many Americans, the word "college" means a four-year degree. The two-year associate's degree gets a bad rap, both in terms of prestige and rigor of the curriculum. In the minds of many, the four-year degree is the only route to a respectable and rewarding career. They want to brag to their friends that Johnny is going to Prestigious Private College or Flagship State U., not Local Community College. To them, community colleges are synonymous with failure.

It's unfortunate that community colleges are often viewed negatively. Many people who go to a four-year college—and often end up dropping out—would be much better off starting or even finishing at a two-year college. Community colleges offer critical building blocks for the modular degree of the future. Their small first-year classes and low cost allow students to explore careers and majors, all while earning valuable credits. Students and parents who have a wide variety of choices about where to go to college are beginning to take notice—25 percent of students from households earning $100,000 or more now attend community colleges, up from 12 percent five years ago.

Community colleges need not be only a building block

to a bachelor's degree—they can be an end in themselves. If you were to consider only the economic return on the credential, associate's degrees pay off too and, in some cases, more than if students went on to get a bachelor's degree. In Colorado, for instance, graduates with an associate's degree in an applied field (think registered nurses and power transmission installers) earn on average around $41,000 a year after graduation, some $8,000 more than those with bachelor's degree (the median per capita income in Colorado is about $31,000).

Indeed, it takes a bachelor's degree recipient in Colorado ten years to out-earn someone with an applied associate's degree, at which point they do so by only a couple of hundred dollars. The story is the same in a handful of other states that have studied the earnings of students after graduation (to see other states, go to http://www.collegemeasures.org/esm). And remember that most of those two-year degrees cost less to begin with, and graduates entered the job market at least two years earlier than graduates of four-year schools.

Americans have a wide variety of choices beyond the bachelor's degree—associate's degrees, occupational certificates, apprenticeships, industry certifications—that are the gateway to a significant proportion of the jobs of tomorrow that won't be easily automated by robots. Most of those are "middle-skills jobs," which demand more than a high school diploma but less than a bachelor's degree. There are roughly 29 million of these jobs today. Some 11 million of them pay $50,000 or more a year, and 4 million pay $75,000 or more. Even though most people think of these as blue-collar jobs, nearly half of them are in office occupations.

Despite the demand, many of these jobs in advanced manufacturing, health care, and information technology remain open because employers can't find qualified candidates to fill them. We often hear the predictions that the United States will face a shortage of computer scientists and engineers in the decade ahead, but rarely do we hear that the nation will also face a shortage of nutritionists, welders, and nurses' aides. Middle schools and high schools have essentially given up on career and technical training, leaving a generation of students who are uninterested in pursuing a four-year academic track without other educational choices. By 2020, at a time when most jobs will require additional or specialized education, it's projected that nearly four in ten U.S. workers will have only a high school diploma or less.

If you're on the fence about pursuing a bachelor's degree or not quite sure what you want to do in life, don't dismiss community college. But know that not all community colleges are created equal. Be sure to check out their transfer rates if your goal is to go on to a four-year college and look at their job-placement rates based on your major if you want a job with your associate's degree. Two-year colleges have a pecking order just like four-year universities. There are the Harvards and Stanfords of community colleges, although their prestige is measured more by how engaged their students are in learning and how connected their academic programs are to the needs of the local economy.

Two-year schools that stand out in serving students who are not blindly following the four-year bachelor's track include Miami Dade and Valencia Colleges in Florida, Santa Barbara City College in California, Saint Paul College in Minnesota, and Kingsborough Community College in Brooklyn. To see what a good community college should look like, I took a trip to one of the best: Walla Walla Community College.

Walla Walla is a charming small town tucked in a valley near the southeast corner of Washington State, thirteen miles north of the Oregon border. For much of its history, agriculture—wheat, strawberries, and sweet onions—defined this town in the shadows of the Cascade Mountains. But in the late 1990s, the agriculture industry began to decline. Technology and complex machinery replaced human labor in the fields and in food-processing factories. Lumber mills were shuttered, leaving the Washington State Penitentiary as the city's largest employer. Soon hundreds of people were arriving at Walla Walla Community College searching for retraining opportunities.

"A lot of laid-off people wanted to retrain, but for what?" said Steven L. VanAusdle, the college's president, who arrived in 1984. "That was a turning point for us, a wake-up call. We looked at what we were doing, and it wasn't good enough for a community that needed our help." The college doubled the size of its nursing program after determining the area could meet the supply. "Then we started looking at what else we could do."

They found answers in the lush rolling fields around the college. The first was in the local wine industry. In 2000, when the college started a degree in enology and viticulture, the region had just sixteen wineries, and the industry was little more than a hobby for many people. Today, there are nearly two hundred local wineries, and they have spawned a vast hospitality sector in the region with restaurants and hotels and a healthy tourist business constrained only by Walla Walla's remote location.

About thirty students enter the community college's enology and viticulture program each year and learn about all aspects of the wine business through College Cellars, an on-campus winery that is open to the public. Every student completes at least one internship before graduation, and many of them work in the industry while going to school. About 60 percent of the graduates, many of them adults who saw this as an on-ramp to a new career, stay in the area.

The second opportunity the college saw in its surrounding fields was in the technologically advanced equipment that had replaced people in agriculture. The machines still needed humans to fix them. The college had a generic mechanics program, but as engines and machinery became more sophisticated by the year, students needed both brawn and brains to get a job. When Andy Winnett started repairing farm tractors for a John Deere dealer in 1977, he told me that all he needed was a toolbox.

"Today your toolbox is a computer," said Winnett, who now directs the John Deere technology program at Walla Walla. John Deere partners with several community colleges around the country to train technicians for its dealer network. At Walla Walla, about fifteen to twenty students come through the program each semester. Because they are sponsored by a John Deere dealer, where the students work for half the program, most graduate in two years with a job in hand. On average, a technician starts at a salary between $31,000 and $39,000 a year, plus bonuses.

I met Winnett outside his office at Walla Walla, where a

lineup of the iconic green John Deere tractors sat idle. The equipment, worth more than a million dollars, was donated by the company for students to practice on. Today's John Deere tractors have at least twenty-four computers embedded in them, mostly focused on emissions. Such advanced machines, however, require technicians with advanced math and comprehension skills, attributes many students interested in the program lack.

Jobs like the ones John Deere offer are still associated in people's minds with students who performed poorly in high school. But the students I found at Walla Walla easily had the academic credentials to get into a four-year college; they'd just rather work with their hands.

Oscar Tapia, a twenty-year-old from Bakersfield, California, told me he had plans to go to a four-year college for an engineering degree but changed his mind when he heard about the John Deere program at a diesel mechanic class while a junior in high school. After he graduates from Walla Walla, he plans to work for the dealer sponsoring him in Bakersfield. Still, he hasn't ruled out getting that four-year engineering degree someday. "I want to show the John Deere engineers how to design a better tractor," he said with a smirk.

For Tapia, the community college was not the destination, but only one stop on what he views as a lifelong trip through education.

Indeed, you should stop thinking of your college education as sitting in a classroom following a script outlined by a course catalog or a professor at the front of a lecture hall. Your education should be a lifelong journey. This is what the author Alvin Toffler observed in the quote that opened this chapter. Our lives will be defined by a journey of *learning, unlearning,* and *relearning.*

New ways of teaching, fueled by the Internet and a diverse band of tech entrepreneurs, cognitive psychologists, artificial intelligence experts, and neuroscientists, are encouraging a radical rethinking of how we learn throughout our lives. After years of talking about how we need to become lifelong learners, the rhetoric has finally reached reality.

CHAPTER 8

EDUCATION, DELIVERED JUST IN TIME

T HE YEAR IS 2018. YOU APPLY TO STANFORD UNI-
VERSITY AND ARE ACCEPTED. BUT INSTEAD OF OF-
FERING YOU THE USUAL FOUR YEARS OF
undergraduate education, Stanford admits you for six years
of study that can be used any time in your life.

This concept may sound radical in the stodgy world of
higher education that hasn't changed in three centuries, but
this "open loop university" was actually developed in 2014
by Stanford's renowned design school as part of a yearlong
exercise by students and faculty to reimagine the college experience.

The idea challenges the concept that an undergraduate
education must take place at one specific time period in a
person's life. With this new model, students could start college when they were ready—at sixteen, eighteen, or twenty-

six years old—and distribute the six years as they saw fit. They could "loop out" after two years to work for a Silicon Valley start-up and then "loop in" a few years later if the start-up failed.

Students who returned after looping out—what the Stanford plan called "populi" who are connected to the university no matter where they live—could use the time that remained on their six-year clock to transition into new careers in their thirties or fifties. These older students with work experience who looped back in would provide inspiration and insight to accelerate research in labs and develop professional partnerships with professors.

Stanford's "open loop" plan raises an interesting question: Why does formal education have an end point in today's world where knowledge is constantly growing and changing?

Already, the informal education that adults have typically cobbled together on their own throughout their lifetime is becoming more formalized and collaborative through activities such as peer discussion groups in online classes and homemade YouTube videos. As working adults feel the necessity of keeping their skills sharp, this networked learning is likely to become more prevalent in the future. While colleges and universities will continue to be places of formal learning for young adults, an array of providers will enable learning in shorter chunks of time, just when recent college graduates need it.

It's called just-in-time education, and it's already happening for millions of twentysomethings.

A Boot Camp for Practical Skills

THE ELEVATOR OPENED ON THE EIGHTH FLOOR OF AN office building two blocks from the White House, revealing what at first looked like a not-quite-finished construction site with concrete floors and open ceilings. On a wall near the reception desk, a campus map listed the locations for "networking," "whiteboarding," "concepting," and "serendipitous conversing." It was certainly cheeky and unlike any other campus map I had ever seen before. But then again, this was not really a typical campus. I had come to General Assembly, a "boot camp" that offers classes in practical skills from web design to social media marketing.

In just its four years of existence, more than 240,000 students have taken individual classes at General Assembly. Each class usually last a few hours and costs anywhere from $30 to $60. Another 12,000 students have paid around $12,000 for full- and part-time, multiweek courses in the fourteen cities where General Assembly operates its "campuses."

I was at General Assembly on a Friday morning a few weeks before Christmas to take one of its short courses, the two-hour "Storytelling for Entrepreneurs: Presentations to Elevator Pitches." I joined about a dozen people who paid forty dollars each to learn how to tell better stories about themselves and their ideas, a seemingly basic skill that, as they went around the room introducing themselves, became clear they hadn't yet learned anywhere else (much like the college graduates I met at Koru).

Several of the students had full-time jobs and were using

the class for professional development. A few were unemployed. The rest had a business idea they wanted to persuade a venture capitalist to put some money behind. Our instructor was a young, rail-thin Berkeley economics graduate who had trained as an improv actor and now used that know-how as a "story coach." Most of the class time was spent paired with another student to practice what we learned in brief sidebar lectures from the instructor. My partner was Allyson Yuen, a lively young woman from California.

Allyson graduated from Whittier College, a private liberal arts school near Los Angeles, in 2011 with a double major in psychology and child development. She was somewhat directionless through college, never totally sure what she wanted to do in life or quite how to figure it out. When she arrived at Whittier, she had her sights set on becoming a teacher but didn't have a major in mind. She chose psychology after taking a few classes. "I was always fascinated by people," Allyson said. "My friends started to take child development classes, and I realized the requirements overlapped, so I added a second major."

She had a brief flirtation with research, but a student teaching gig at a middle school in the spring of her senior year convinced her she wanted to be in a classroom with students rather than tucked away in a lab. A career counselor at Whittier suggested she apply to AmeriCorps, the national service program, so she did and was accepted. Three months after graduation, she set off for Denver, where she helped low-income eighth graders improve their reading and math skills.

Allyson felt that AmeriCorps gave her the hands-on experience she never really got in college. But now she was at a loss for what to do next. Being in school had always provided her with that next thing, but she was having trouble navigating on her own. Even so, she pushed ahead and took a series of random turns and detours over the next two years: a two-month unpaid internship in Chicago, a stint as an administrative assistant back home to California, another unpaid internship in Washington, D.C., and then a job as a marketing manager at a tech company in California.

Now she was back in Washington and once again on the job hunt. She signed up for this class to help her frame her career narrative in job interviews. This was her second General Assembly class in less than a week. Previously she had paid thirty-five dollars for an hour-and-a-half class—"Look Before You Leap: Making the Career Switch"—even though she didn't have a career yet. General Assembly provided a somewhat formal learning environment where she didn't have to invest years of her life or thousands of her dollars in a university degree or certificate, but could still connect with a network and learn a skill.

Three and a half years after graduating from college, Allyson was still looking for both meaningful work and a steady paycheck. She had just celebrated her twenty-fifth birthday. Allyson was a Wanderer. She wasn't that different from one of the founders of General Assembly when he was her age.

Finding the On-Ramp to a Career After College

NEARLY EVERY START-UP BEGINS WHEN SOMEONE FACES A problem, figures out a solution, and turns that fix into a new company for others facing similar issues. That's how Jake Schwartz came to start General Assembly. He told me his story as we were standing on a street corner in Austin, Texas, one March day.

We were both there for the South by Southwest education conference, an annual gathering that brings together thousands of people interested in what's next in education. Schwartz was taking me on a somewhat circuitous route to the local campus of General Assembly, so he would have enough time to retrace his own meandering path from college to his current career.

Schwartz grew up on a farm in rural Oregon, a good student who had a knack for taking standardized tests. That helped him get into Yale University, where he picked a very general major, American studies. While his friends at Yale zeroed in on jobs with investment banks or big consulting firms, Schwartz wasn't interested in either. He thought that having a piece of paper from an Ivy League institution would open the doors to almost any job he wanted.

"I was totally out to lunch," Schwartz said about his career planning while in college. He didn't do any internships, nor was he deeply engaged with any campus activities.

"I didn't get the game. I literally thought that being a smart Ivy League grad, I'd go into job interviews, and they'd be falling over themselves wanting to hire me."

But that didn't happen, and in his twenties, Schwartz bounced around from job to job. First, he managed a songwriter, then oversaw a nonprofit performing arts space, and at one point summarized medical records for a law firm that specialized in hip-replacement lawsuits.

"I felt like I was a failure," he told me. "I didn't know where my career was going."

He had missed the on-ramp to a career from Yale, and now he thought he couldn't find another entrance without returning to school. At age twenty-six, he pressed the reset button and enrolled in the MBA program at Wharton.

What he found at Penn surprised him. Most of his classmates were equally unhappy, although many of them already had lucrative careers. "Half the people were bankers who wanted to be consultants, and the other half were consultants who wanted to be bankers," he said.

Schwartz said he learned everything he needed from his MBA in the first half of the first semester. He describes the next two and half years as nothing more than networking for jobs and partying. The experience left him frustrated and angry. First off, he had to get an MBA just to get back on the on-ramp to a career. Then he had to spend three years of his twenties and some $200,000 of his grandfather's money when fifteen weeks would have sufficed. His time at Wharton greatly shaped his thinking about General Assembly.

The initial business plan for General Assembly called for a clubhouse for entrepreneurs in New York City, a place where they could hang out and work on their ideas, much like the lounge or common room of a college dorm. The company also offered a few tech classes on the side. When those courses quickly sold out, General Assembly added more of them. As the classes became more popular, the company shifted its business model to that of a school, with locations around the world to fill the almost insatiable demand among twentysomethings who already have a bachelor's degree and are looking for continuing education that will help land them a job.

Investors flocked to the company, backing the start-up with more than $50 million in venture capital. They recognized what recent college graduates had already discovered: that General Assembly provided a cheaper alternative to traditional graduate school to prepare them for jobs in high-demand fields.

The New Version of Graduate School

A DECADE AGO, RECENT GRADUATES NOW ATTENDING General Assembly would have gone back to college for a part-time graduate certificate or a professional master's degree in fields such as communications, marketing, or computer science. Some would have enrolled in business school or law school. Their answer to differentiating themselves in a job market crowded with bachelor's degrees was to get yet *more college.*

Historically, a master's degree was seen as a stop along the way to earning a doctorate and eventually a teaching or research position in academia. But in recent decades, master's degrees in professional areas from nursing to forensic sciences to public administration became cash cows for universities, serving students who thought they needed another credential to get a job. Many of these graduate programs suffered the same curriculum creep as their undergraduate counterparts, as faculty members overloaded them with unnecessary course requirements and, in the process, drove up their cost.

Until the likes of General Assembly came along, students didn't have much of a choice but to pay tens of thousands of dollars for a master's degree. Many students took on debt on top of their undergraduate loans to finance their graduate education. We often hear about recent graduates with $100,000 in debt and assume it is from a bachelor's degree. But less than 1 percent of undergraduates owe a six-figure debt when they graduate, while some 15 percent of graduate students owe at least $100,000 when they're done with school. Overall, student loan debt has doubled since 2008, to some $1.19 trillion today, and 40 percent of that debt is held by graduate students, although they represent just 14 percent of students in higher education.

Even with a master's degree, finding a good, high-paying job was increasingly difficult after the 2008 recession. As a result, the number of American students enrolling in graduate school has been on the decline since 2011 (though overall enrollment is up because of international students).

But more than the hefty price tag is turning students off from the idea of graduate school. There is a fundamental transformation under way in how recent college graduates supplement their education before starting a career. Rather than plug into the formal learning structure of traditional higher education, new graduates are increasingly turning to a new set of providers that offer education in short spurts, online or in face-to-face classes, for a fraction of the cost of graduate school (or in some cases free). These providers are hardly household names, but they are already attracting millions of students. There are three types of players in this new arena:

Boot Camps

In addition to General Assembly's courses in web development, there are some sixty-three coding boot camps operating in the United States and Canada. They teach basic programming skills to students who typically don't have previous experience. It remains unclear whether the boot camp model can easily translate to other career fields, where there isn't as much demand for workers who are willing to foot the typical $11,000 bill for these programs. For now, students can't use federal financial aid dollars for boot camps. However, the U.S. Department of Education is considering a partnering arrangement with existing colleges to tap into federal aid.

Massive Open Online Courses (MOOCs)

Several dozen elite universities, including Stanford, Princeton, Penn, and Harvard, offer free online courses through two major organizations, Coursera and edX. More than one hundred thousand people have signed up for some of these classes, which span a variety of topics. MOOCs have attracted criticism in recent years because only about one in ten students completes an entire course. But applying the traditional measures of how we define success in higher education to this new way of learning misses what many of the students I interviewed told me was their reasons for taking the classes. Some enroll to try out a course or they want to watch a particular lecture for its content. They never planned to complete the course, and it was free so they have nothing to lose when they stop taking it.

Digital Learning Resources

The web is full of DIY education sites, from YouTube to iTunes U, where students can piece together their own curriculum. Some of these sites have more visitors in one month than universities have students over an entire century. The Khan Academy, for instance, serves some 10 million people a month with five thousand videos. Lynda.com, an online education company, reaches more than 4 million people a year with its how-to tutorials in everything from management skills to programming.

Not a Degree, but the Foundational Knowledge to Start a Job

BOOT CAMPS HAVE A SIMPLE GOAL: TO GET YOU A JOB. General Assembly claims 90 percent of its graduates find work within six months. Another coding academy, the Flatiron School, had an independent auditor study its job-placement rates and found that 95 percent of graduates were placed in a job within four months.

There is no tension between theory and practice in boot camps. It's all about vocational training, done as quickly as possible. Everything in a typical undergraduate or graduate curriculum that employers see as irrelevant is discarded. One computer science instructor at General Assembly boasted that its ten-week program is equivalent to what an undergraduate learns in a four-year bachelor's degree.

Just-in-time education is like basic training in the military, in that it gives you the foundational knowledge to get started. Everything else will be learned on the job or perhaps in another course down the road.

Because General Assembly, Coursera, and Lynda.com are focused on teaching only job-relevant skills, they operate in a narrow space that makes it fairly easy for them to claim success. There is demand for their classes and easy-to-measure outcomes—graduates either get a job or they don't. In some ways it's difficult to compare them with traditional graduate programs because they don't have the full breadth of offerings and probably never will. Still, the short course I took on storytelling at General Assembly was helpful to my work and, more important, was a low risk on my part. I didn't have to navigate a campus or commit to a semester-long class, and all it cost me was the price of a ticket to a football game at a big university.

But some students take a bigger risk at General Assembly. R. J. Dabber enrolled in the ten-week, $3,500 web-development class. He told me he felt he didn't have much of a choice if he wanted get a job as a coder. He graduated in 2012 with a math degree from Wesleyan University and thought his background in a STEM field was a ticket to a job. But R.J. had little interest in pursuing a career in finance, banking, or insurance, and he later discovered that's where the money and the jobs are when you're a math major.

After graduation, he worked for a friend developing a mobile app and realized he had a knack for computer coding.

He applied for a few jobs in New York City, but when he went to interviews, he quickly recognized that he was woefully underqualified. Unlike many first jobs right out of school where smart college graduates might persuade managers to hire them, when armed with a degree in computer programming from a top university, it is all about whether you can code. The degree doesn't really matter.

"I took a few computer science classes in college to fulfill math requirements, but they were taught in Basic code," R.J. told me. "No one codes in Basic."

A friend told him about General Assembly. He signed up for the first available course, which his parents paid for. "It was kind of ridiculous that I just paid $200,000 for a degree, and there was nothing like this at Wesleyan that I could have taken that would have prepared me for work like GA's course did," he said.

Near the end of his General Assembly class, R.J. started to apply for jobs. He added his code to GitHub, a website that allowed him to share what he did at General Assembly with potential employers. He also put General Assembly at the top of his résumé, above Wesleyan. A few months after he finished the General Assembly class, he got a job at a Brooklyn-based web-development firm. His boss, who had dropped out of college, didn't even know R.J. had a degree from Wesleyan until several weeks after he started the job.

The potential market for continuing education after college is enormous. Employers spend $413 billion on informal, on-the-job training annually, and individuals spend another $30 billion for professional education and certification. The new providers of just-in-time education excel at feeding chunks of content to students instead of giving them a full helping of a degree or a certificate when they don't need it and can't afford it.

The other advantage is that their curriculum is designed according to how the brain actually learns: lectures in short time blocks only, a focus on a few key concepts, immediate application of learning in a real-world environment, frequent feedback—all completed in a few weeks. Then the process is repeated with a new set of concepts. It's exactly the opposite of the structure of most colleges.

Employers are also seeing how just-in-time education can benefit their own workplaces. Take Xerox, for instance. In the 1970s, the company opened a massive campus in suburban Washington, D.C., to train its global sales and management workforce. Some 1,800 employees would come through the facility in any given week for classes. But Xerox sold the campus and now conducts most of its training virtually, every day, with more than 10,000 short, web-based videos and another 20,000 on-demand reference materials. Today, 70 percent of Xerox training is online.

Online education saves the company money, but according to John Leutner, Xerox's head of global learning, it also improves retention because workers learn on their own time and at their own pace. "We think too much of education as having a beginning and an end," he said. "We need to think about learning more iteratively and in milestones."

The question is if education becomes a lifelong pursuit, will starting the bachelor's degree at age eighteen always be as important as it is today? In other words, if you will need access to learning for the rest of your life, should you continue to focus so intensely on going to school for four years during this sometimes confusing transition time in your life? To find the answer, I went to a place I often turn to when confronted with questions about the connection between higher education and the economy: Georgetown University's Center on Education and the Workforce.

A New Phase of the Twenties: Learning and Earning

THE CENTER IS HOUSED IN AN OFFICE BUILDING A FEW blocks north of Georgetown's main campus and hidden behind the British School of Washington, a tony private institution on Wisconsin Avenue. The center is run by Tony Carnevale, a gruff, old-school government policy maker who came of age as a Washington economist during the 1970s.

On the October day I met him in his office, the numbers on his mind weren't the latest unemployment figures released that morning by the Department of Labor, but rather the available parking spaces in his building's underground garage. Parents of the students at the British School had rented spaces so they could have a warm and dry place to drop off their kids each morning. That meant there were fewer spaces for employees in the building to lease, although the parents parked for just a few minutes each day. "And then we wonder why kids aren't ready for work," Carnevale said to me with a sigh. "Because they aren't allowed to get wet in kindergarten."

While it's conventional wisdom to think that over the last three decades parenting and schools have made children more risk averse, Carnevale believes the nature of risk has changed. Today's economy is much more treacherous for workers than for previous generations, and college is no longer the linear pathway to guaranteed success; a few wrong moves can make the difference between heading off to a great job or standing in the unemployment line. So parents, especially high-income parents, want to give their children every advantage in this race, including shielding them from raindrops in kindergarten.

Though he can joke about the private school parents, Carnevale isn't focused on elementary students or even high school students. He's worried about what happens when those kindergartners eventually make their way into the workplace.

Every year, the Georgetown center produces a steady stream of reports about the value of college credentials in the labor market, and the reports garner plenty of media attention for their headline-grabbing statistics. If you read enough of them, you'll conclude that the nation's patchwork education system is seriously outdated for preparing the workforce in this new economy.

From his perch in the nation's capital, Carnevale frequently deals with politicians and the rhetoric that reflects the anxiety their constituents are feeling about the fragile economy, particularly the decline of middle-class jobs. In large part that worry stems from the public clinging to a nostalgia for the post–World War II economic boom that brought a wave of college-educated GIs into the workforce, saw factories operating at full capacity, and, most of all, experienced little competition from overseas or from technology.

Carnevale points out that the economic effects of World War II finally ran out of steam in the early 1970s. That's when higher education became absolutely critical to the success of twentysomethings, especially young men who had fewer options for blue-collar jobs if they skipped college altogether. Building on the body of research that found adolescents delaying their move into adulthood, Carnevale studied several decades of labor statistics and discovered the same trend in the job market. The march into a career for new college graduates has been slowing down since the 1980s. And the 2008 economic crisis finally exposed the malaise that had been facing young people for a while.

"It is clear from the evidence that today's generation of youth bore the brunt of the economic shocks during the first decade of the 21st century," Carnevale wrote in a groundbreaking 2013 report from the center, called *Failure to Launch*. "Everyone suffered, but young people tend to be more vulnerable to the cyclical economic fluctuations than other age groups."

Page after page of the report lays out a series of worrisome numbers about young Americans. In 2013, the employment rate for adults in their twenties had reached its lowest level since the government started collecting data in the early 1950s. The net worth of individuals under the age of thirty-five had declined by nearly 70 percent since the early 1980s. Among all the findings was one that elicited perhaps the most angst when I'd mention it to students and parents: young workers are taking longer to reach employment rates equal to those of their counterparts of earlier generations.

To Carnevale, these numbers represent a momentous change in how and when we learn, and how and when we work. Historically workers have entered the labor market at age eighteen and left at age sixty-four, but that is no longer a reality, and it hasn't been for a while. Yet every day parents and the American education system prepare students for that model.

To illustrate his point, Carnevale drew three boxes in a straight line: education, work, and retirement. Those were the phases of life when he was growing up. The picture today is more jumbled. He added several other boxes on the page after education and before retirement. He circled one of them several times, what he called "learning and earning." That is the period when young people are in their twenties and developing their "human capital" by going to graduate school, finding internships and fellowships, working part-time, or, increasingly, navigating the alternative learning economy.

Carnevale sees nothing wrong with the Wanderers and Stragglers taking their twenties to "figure things out" as long as they continue to invest in their human capital by working in relevant jobs or taking classes to improve their skills. But Carnevale's diagram still had boxes for college or a similar credential at the beginning of this new phase of learning and earning. That answered the question I wanted to ask when I first came to his office.

No matter what, he said, a college degree remains the foundation of lifelong education, though some degrees are much more valuable than others. Every year, the center produces a report that explores the financial payoff of different college majors—how much students earn and their chances of being unemployed. Its analysis has found, not surprisingly, that humanities majors earn a lot less than science majors and are more likely to be unemployed. A degree in art or psychology pays $31,000 right out of college, while one in engineering pays $57,000.

Though he's not advocating that students pick a major based solely on what they might earn someday or the risk of being unemployed, Carnevale said the information is none-theless important to consider because in his opinion some majors are equivalent to choosing an occupation these days. A generic college degree was useful in the past because in-dustries mattered more than specific jobs, and employers were willing to train their workers. You could work your way up through an employer, like David Taylor did. He's the new CEO of Procter & Gamble, who started with the com-pany in the early 1980s as a production manager and moved through different occupations within the firm on his way to the corner office.

But career paths like that are rare today. Nowadays, you pick an occupation after a few years of what the economist Henry Siu describes as "occupational shopping" and move through different industries throughout your career.

Graduate and professional schools, however, were built on the old model. Their job was to provide students the deep specialization needed after a general education at the under-graduate level. But employers now expect both broad and deep learning to come packaged with the bachelor's degree—the T-shaped individual. They want learners who can adapt throughout their careers and learn on the spot when needed.

That's why General Assembly's classes are selling out. It's considered a fast detour around graduate school for people who just need a specific skill to get a job. It's also why officials at Georgetown are designing a new degree that flattens the traditional firewall between undergraduate and graduate degrees.

The idea of just-in-time education has the potential to completely wipe away the line marking the end of college and the beginning of one's working life. Increasingly, students are unwilling to pay for expensive graduate degrees when much cheaper alternatives like General Assembly exist.

A few weeks after I met up with Schwartz in Austin, George Washington University announced that it was laying off employees to reduce costs. The university's president blamed a decline in enrollment in graduate and professional programs. That same week LinkedIn announced it was buying Lynda.com for $1.5 billion, almost double George Washington University's annual budget.

LinkedIn has some 300 million members, and the company knows what skills they need in order to get the jobs advertised on its own website—skills offered by Lynda.com. LinkedIn could help job applicants bypass the traditional higher education system altogether in finding employment. Lynda.com would provide online training, while LinkedIn would suggest specific classes based on the jobs its members are browsing on the site.

Employers remain the other big force in shifting our notion of when college ends. If employers in industries other than technology send the signal to job seekers that skills learned in the real world matter more than an undergraduate or a master's degree, companies like General Assembly will adapt their model for other occupations.

Schwartz told me he's already thinking of how General Assembly could offer programs in health care. Other occupations would eventually follow, and the gated entrance to a career that universities now largely control would open for anyone at any time throughout their lifetime.

CHAPTER 9

HOW EMPLOYERS HIRE

"HOW DO YOU HIRE?"
The question was simple enough, and I asked everyone I met in start-ups and small firms to nonprofit organizations to Fortune 500 companies. I wanted to find out what employers look for in today's young adults—along with how and where they find it.

Surprisingly, employers often didn't know what they wanted, revealing a level of dysfunction for matching talent and opportunity that I didn't expect in an economy as advanced as that of the United States. I learned that employers fail to plan very far in advance for their hiring needs, evaluate candidates during interviews based largely on gut instinct, and rely heavily on the halo effect of credentials from a small set of elite schools.

Even now when companies can measure and track everything about their businesses in precise analytical terms—

from how many boxes of laundry detergent they sell on Tuesdays in Topeka to the last time their top salesperson called a client—employers' relationships with their workers and, more important, with potential talent are remarkably casual in nature.

No wonder twentysomethings on the job market describe the hiring process as a "black box" that keeps them in the dark about where they stand and what skills they need to be hired. The application and interview practices at most organizations are far from transparent, especially for young adults applying for their first real job. As Peter Cappelli, a professor at the Wharton School, has written, "hiring doesn't seem to be as big a priority for U.S. employers as it was a generation ago."

Although no two workplaces hire in exactly the same way, I found similarities among organizations within industries, regions of the country, and company size. For the most part, the hiring process for new college graduates adheres to a traditional playbook that relies heavily on personal interactions (technology is beginning to play a larger role, and we'll look at that later in the chapter).

Most big companies still travel to campus recruiting events each year at a group of "core schools" they have identified. They decide on which schools to visit based on where they have found success in the past—usually defined by the numbers of students who accepted job offers, not necessarily those who were the best match. The largest of the companies or those that hire thousands of graduates a year tend to divide their lineup of schools into several tiers (the higher the tier, the more visits they typically make).

The main way a school gets to the top of the list is based

primarily on the prevalence of relevant majors and the school's ranking, according to an annual survey by the National Association of Colleges and Employers. Even so, I discovered that putting together the target list is more art than science. A school is sometimes considered core because the CEO went there or is a trustee, or the hiring manager is a graduate.

But what should matter most to students on the job market is not which organizations send recruiters to campus, but which ones make the most job offers. In the end, it's the job that counts, and the highest offer rates, the survey of employers found, went to graduates of schools where executives were alumni and the salary expectations of new employees were in sync with the hiring company.

Some employers, such as Wall Street banks, consulting companies, international brands, and some tech companies, keep their list of target schools deliberately small. They see hiring as an extension of their gold-plated brands, and they tend to recruit only from the very top of the college rankings. "If you don't go to a top twenty-five university, you'll never see a recruiter from some companies," a former president at a well-known public university once told me. "The schools outside the top tier will never tell prospective students that. They make it seem like you can get hired anywhere, but you can't."

So if you don't go to a highly selective college, does that mean you're destined for a second-rate job at a mediocre company? Not at all. I hope this book has shown you that what you *do in college* is more important than where you *go to college.* It is possible to get a job with a company even if it doesn't recruit on your campus, but it will be more challenging to penetrate its recruiting machine. And be prepared for disappointment: certain employers will reject you based solely on which school you attended.

When it comes to hiring, employers are not always consistent. Recall the recruiter from Procter & Gamble who favored graduates from large public universities, while the company's CEO touted liberal arts graduates. Indeed, companies tend to favor large public flagship universities, if for no other reason than they produce scores of graduates each spring. In 2010, the *Wall Street Journal* asked recruiters at nearly five hundred of the largest companies, nonprofits, and government agencies which schools they liked the best and trusted the most when looking for new college graduates. The top five? Penn State, Texas A&M, the University of Illinois, Purdue, and Arizona State—all public universities. The only private school in the top ten was Carnegie Mellon (at number ten) and the only Ivy League institution in the top twenty-five was Cornell, at number fourteen.

Despite the differences I found in how employers hire, the college degree—whether an associate's or a bachelor's—is still the initial screening device for nearly all organizations when they sort through potential recruits. That is why so many American families extend themselves to pay for a college education. But whether the degree will remain as strong in the future is unclear, as employers find better ways to locate and evaluate talent.

An analysis by Burning Glass found that one in five non–health care job ads requiring a bachelor's degree also called for a certificate or license, which means that employers see the college degree "as a minimum ticket to ride rather than something validating specific competencies," according to Matthew Sigelman, the company's CEO. As a result, college students shouldn't depend just on their degree, even one from a prestigious university, as their only ticket to landing a job after graduation.

How Campus Recruiting Has Changed

PHIL GARDNER, DIRECTOR OF THE COLLEGIATE EMPLOY-ment Research Institute at Michigan State University, has spent more than thirty years observing how companies recruit new college graduates. He spends a good part of his year on the road, speaking at campus career centers to update his colleagues on the advice they should be dispensing to undergraduates.

I met Gardner before a talk at the University of Maryland Career Center. I asked him how campus recruiting has changed and what that means for students about to go on the job market. Gardner described three main developments that make the road from college to career more treacherous now than it was for graduates even a decade ago.

First, he said, the size and makeup of companies recruiting on campuses has shifted, altering the entire hiring process. In the 1980s, campus recruiting was dominated by three primary industries—manufacturing, retail, and finance—and a few big corporations controlled each of those sectors. That meant the big employers set the recruiting calendar, and everyone else followed along. It was an easy process for both students and campuses to understand and plug into. In 1985, GM and Dow Chemical, combined, hired 340 Michigan State graduates, Gardner told me. But in 2014, those two companies hired only 32 students from Michigan State.

There are more employers today, each of them recruiting fewer students, and all have specific needs and different timetables for students to keep track of. Companies that build things no longer dominate the economy; business and professional services that reorganize those old-line companies now do. Nonprofit and government agencies also loom over hiring in a way they didn't in the past. Teach for America and AmeriCorps are among the top ten destinations for Michigan State graduates today, and several other nonprofit organizations fill spots in the top fifteen. In the 1980s, none of those spots was occupied by nonprofit groups. In a nationwide survey, more than 40 percent of the class of 2014 said they wanted to work for the government, either at the federal, state, or local level.

Second, employers have raised the bar on the skills workers need to start a job on day one and are less involved in employee training. Young adults are largely on their own to acquire those skills. Doing so becomes increasingly challenging because the rules keep shifting. Only a quarter of companies have specific hiring targets when they start campus recruiting, according to surveys by Gardner's institute. Workplaces are engaging in more on-demand or last-minute hiring, so students can't know even months in advance what they need to know for a job, let alone before signing up for classes or before picking a major.

"We're asking twenty-three-year-old new graduates to

act like thirty-five-year-old experienced workers," Gardner said.

In the old days, Fortune 500 companies put new hires into "rotational programs" that allowed them to move around different departments to learn about the company and its culture, as well as various jobs. Many of those programs have been eliminated in corporate cost cutting.

The third major development, according to Gardner, is the increased velocity of today's economy. Entire industries have been disrupted by technology and globalization in recent years, even stalwarts like law, accounting, and medicine. Yet colleges are under more pressure than ever to help their students find precise routes into careers when those routes don't exist anymore.

In a 2015 survey, two-thirds of college leaders said that more discussions about job preparation were occurring on their campuses compared with just three years earlier. But what kinds of jobs are campuses supposed to be preparing students for? How does anyone know what the job market might look like in two or four years?

Entire industries are disappearing almost overnight, and legacy companies are quickly changing course. In one recent year, Gardner told me, Procter & Gamble hired graduates from eighty-six different majors at Michigan State, reflecting both its new lines of business and its eagerness to hedge its bets to find the right match. Giving solid career advice to a bunch of twenty-two-year-olds seems about as safe a bet as picking stocks or trying to win at roulette.

After we finished breakfast, I walked across the campus to the university's career center to watch Gardner's presentation. As I passed undergraduates, I wondered how many of them were aware of the depth of the changes in the job market that they would soon confront.

Colleges rarely sound the alarm for undergraduates about the difficulty of getting a job after graduation, especially for those who are on their way to becoming Wanderers and Stragglers. Students hear only good news from campus career offices, such as around 90 percent of new graduates are employed. To get to that number, colleges survey their graduates six months after college graduation, and nearly half of schools never ask their graduates that question again. Few colleges examine the percentage of students who found jobs but are underemployed or find out what happens to them five or ten years after graduation. Either universities don't know the answer or they don't want anyone else to know.

Getting to the Job Offer

HIRING HAS ALWAYS BEEN A LENGTHY AND IMPRECISE practice. In the 1950s, large corporations tried to streamline the process by giving applicants a series of psychological and intelligence tests. By the 1990s, however, companies had abandoned such tests, claiming they were too expensive and ineffective. Instead, the pendulum swung in the completely opposite direction to the subjective and qualitative process we mostly have today, where employers use a variety of sorting mechanisms at different points to narrow the field of candidates.

There are a number of ways that employers sift and sort through prospective job applicants. The first sort happens at the top of the funnel and is largely based on the materials submitted by the candidate (the cover letter, résumé, and application) or what exists in the public domain, such as a LinkedIn profile. At smaller companies, real people still review those materials, giving them a cursory glance to determine the candidate's fit for a position.

But at larger organizations that first cut is increasingly outsourced to applicant tracking software. It searches for key words in the job seeker's materials and automatically discards those missing the necessary requirements, all without the intervention of a real person. At some companies, this software is so finely tuned that it dismisses the vast majority of candidates, even those who could actually do the job.

In his book *Will College Pay Off?*, Cappelli told a story about a basic engineering job where the applicant tracking software rated *none* of the twenty-five thousand job seekers as qualified. This leads Cappelli to doubt the claim that a lack in applicant skills is the cause for persistent unemployment. The problem, he believes, is that employers don't see that certain tasks could be performed in different ways by different people.

For students, getting around the applicant tracking software is nearly impossible. It helps if you can meet a real person who can keep a lookout for your application. If that's not possible, parse the key words from the job ad, especially those words not commonly found in job ads because they can indicate skills that are important to an employer. Then use those key words in your cover letter and résumé.

The second sorting is the interview. At most companies, this is a highly subjective process, done mainly by managers with no experience or training in interviewing or hiring. For entry-level jobs, the interview is typically a half-day or daylong affair with a series of one-on-one conversations with different people in the organization who may have prepared very little and usually ask a random set of questions. As a result, many new college graduates are left disappointed by the interview.

Such unstructured conversations have been found by researchers to be highly ineffective. That's why companies known for their successful hiring practices, such as Google, instead use structured interviews where candidates are asked a consistent list of questions by everyone they meet with clear guidelines for assessing their responses.

"This is the only way we know if the difference between job candidates is because of *their* performance rather than the performance of the interviewer," Laszlo Bock, senior vice president of people operations at Google, told me.

Graduates being interviewed obviously have no say over how the conversation is structured, but there are ways to control the narrative arc of the story you present to an interviewer, which we will explore in the next chapter.

Considering the time, money, and effort companies spend on recruiting new college graduates, it's shocking how little attention they pay to how their interviews are conducted. Lauren A. Rivera, a professor at Northwestern University's Kellogg School of Management, found that this nonchalant approach to interviewing is perhaps most persistent at some of the most prestigious firms where the people *are* the product.

For two years, Rivera embedded herself in the hiring process of some of the highest-paying entry-level jobs—positions at top-tier investment banks, management consulting firms, and law firms. Rivera interviewed more than one hundred people involved in hiring at the firms and candidates who went through the process. Rivera was also able to observe firsthand how one of these firms recruited at an elite college over the course of an entire hiring cycle.

The result was her 2015 book, *Pedigree: How Elite Students Get Elite Jobs*. The book illustrates the random nature of hiring and the hidden bias that crawls into any decision where people are involved. Rivera found that the affiliations of applicants—where they went to school, where they interned or worked previously, or the power of their network—heavily influenced whether they made it into the interview room in the first place. The sheen of a diploma from a top school boosted even poor applicants, and recruiters rarely looked at grades, which they largely distrusted. Extracurricular activities were much more important to them.

Once in the interview, another set of factors came into play, the biggest of which was a fuzzy term we all use, called "fit." In most cases, interviewers wanted to hire people like themselves, applicants with whom they shared a certain chemistry, in the same way you might evaluate someone you're on a date with, or someone you would want to be stuck next to in an airport during a lengthy delay. This is why extracurricular activities mattered second only to alma mater to interviewers. Rapport with a candidate often came through shared activities, such as travel or sports.

At one hiring committee meeting Rivera attended, she watched as a law partner who was a Red Sox fan reject a candidate because he was a Yankees fan. Over and over again, hiring managers told Rivera they were looking for a certain "polish," candidates who would "show well," although the managers often had difficulty defining what they meant. Despite lack of agreement on what those terms mean, employers regularly dismissed applicants who had insufficient polish and who might stand out in a negative way with clients who were older and had more experience.

"Polish consisted of seeming at ease while putting the interviewer at ease," Rivera wrote, "taking the reins in conversation while maintaining adherence to conversational rhythms and turn-taking norms, displaying excitement but keeping it within bounds, and seeming confident yet not cocky."

Rivera noted that some interviewers were told *what* to look for in candidates but were given little or no guidance on *how* to evaluate what they heard or observed. Left on their own, the interviewers focused on hiring people they'd prefer to work with rather than hiring people who would be good at the organization. The hiring practices she described resonated with many of the recent graduates I met who were struggling to launch after college (and probably with anyone who has ever applied for a job).

For employers, this process was resulting in plenty of bad matches. New hires were unhappy and unfulfilled, and it was showing in their performance or they were bolting after a few years. One global report on hiring found that two out of every three new college graduates spent less than five hours researching their current employer when they had applied for the job, and only one in four said they understood the day-to-day work before starting a job.

Companies are beginning to realize their hiring practices aren't always yielding the best candidates, and more of them are beginning to approach hiring as a science and are embracing new technology and data analytics in making their talent decisions. This shift away from the human equation in hiring could transform how students find employment coming out of college and forever change the value of the degree as the sole signaling device that someone is job ready.

How People Analytics Is Changing the Game

IT'S CALLED "PEOPLE ANALYTICS." IN 2014, PENN'S Wharton School hosted a sold-out conference on the topic. I went the next year, and while standing in the taxi line at the hotel, I found myself next to (well, in the shadow of) the six-foot-eight Shane Battier. The former NBA star and Duke basketball standout was a headliner at the conference because he was once described by the author Michael Lewis as the "No-Stats All-Star."

Teams simply were better when Battier was on the court. Lewis is also the author of *Moneyball,* the bestselling book and the hit movie, which told the story of how the Oakland Athletics used player data to field an inexpensive, yet competitive, Major League Baseball team. Human resources offices at major companies have realized in recent years that their employees are a lot like the talent on a baseball field or a basketball court, so they have begun to harness thousands of pieces of data to figure out why and how their workers are hired, fired, and promoted. That was the birth of people analytics. Today, 4,500 companies have at least one employee focused on people analytics; half the companies created those positions just after 2010.

At lunch I sat with William Wolf, the head of talent acquisition and development at Credit Suisse. He had been recruited to the global banking firm in 2010 to establish its people analytics team. One of his early goals was to study hiring successes to see how possible it was to identify recruits who will "survive and thrive." As he defined it, those are employees who stay for more than two years and perform well in their jobs. The bank had a number of new hires that didn't pan out. Meanwhile, others who had summer internships there had turned down full-time job offers in favor of positions at other banks, tech firms, or private equity firms. Bank officials were worried they were getting a reputation as a place where new hires failed or didn't stay very long.

"With all of the challenges we face in the market for top university recruits, hiring mistakes can end up harming our brand," Wolf told me.

Wolf's team tried to determine whether there are experiences in a student's background that could better predict success at the company. His team looked at dozens of variables on résumés and in the screening process and asked a series of questions: Do athletes outperform nonathletes? They don't. Does evidence of accomplishment in music matter? It doesn't among undergraduates, but sustained accomplishment among graduate students does. Foreign language competency? Does not help.

Some of the answers led to changes in Credit Suisse's screening and interviewing process. For example, historically the bank had emphasized quantitative reasoning in hiring given the number of calculations young bankers do every day. So it tended to favor applicants with high GMAT scores, SAT math scores, and college GPAs. But the data team discovered that attributes like leadership counted for much more than expected, and the bank developed new scoring guidelines that emphasized leadership across the board, but not just any leadership position. For example, students who had earned the top spot through skill or dedication, such as a captain of a varsity athletic team, were more likely to succeed than those popularly elected, say to student government.

I asked Wolf whether the data could better inform his list of top target schools. He acknowledged that campus hiring is still done by an army of volunteer screeners and interviewers who apply their own judgment to candidates. So a student with a 3.8 GPA from Big State U. may be asked tougher questions than a student with a similar GPA from an Ivy League school because the interviewer applies a higher standard, thinking that hiring the Big State U. candidate is a risk. Thus it's difficult to say if hires from one school perform better than those from another given the different human filters.

"Our team tries to improve the judgment of recruiters by arming them with analytical information when it appears their biases have led to poor decisions," Wolf explained.

Wolf hopes that by emphasizing data and results over traditional biases recruiters will become more confident about hiring students from nontraditional schools. Over time, he believes, the school name on the diploma will matter less to hiring managers. Already, by using virtual recruiting, the bank is hiring from a broader range of schools and that helps Credit Suisse reach more students who want to make banking a long-term career choice, not a ticket to be punched on the way to a hedge fund job.

The data that Wolf and his team at Credit Suisse is analyzing still relies on the traditional measures of aptitude listed on résumés and college transcripts, including GPA, extracurricular activities, and internships. But the future of what people analytics might mean for new college graduates goes well beyond those traditional measures. It is being built by Guy Halfteck, the founder of a Silicon Valley start-up called Knack, which makes video games for your smartphone. I downloaded one of them, Wasabi Waiter, at the Penn conference and was instantly hooked.

But Knack's games are not purely for entertainment; they measure the users' resourcefulness, numerical reasoning, and risk taking. In Wasabi Waiter, my task was to deliver sushi orders based on the facial expressions of a growing number of customers who suddenly appeared on my screen. I had to give them the menu, deliver a lineup of food from meals piling up in the kitchen, and clear dishes. Meanwhile, behind the scenes, the game was tracking my every move and noting how well I prioritize, solve problems, and learn from mistakes—all skills employers want. Indeed, in just ten to twenty minutes, the game collected enough information to make an assessment of my abilities.

Naturally, I was skeptical that a game I had just downloaded to my smartphone revealed more about my potential in just a few minutes than a four-hour SAT test. Others were just as dubious when they first heard of Knack, including the head of Royal Dutch Shell's innovation team, known as the GameChanger unit. As Don Peck first reported in the *Atlantic* magazine, the petroleum giant wanted to figure out how to find the best ideas of the hundreds proposed by employees in order to bring them to the market more quickly. The company decided to run an experiment with Knack.

Shell asked about 900 of 1,400 employees who, over the years, had generated ideas to play two of the games and also told Knack how well those people had performed as idea generators. With both pieces of information in hand, Knack developed profiles of people who had the good ideas and those who had weak ideas. The remaining 500 employees also played the game, but Knack had to guess if they had proposed breakthrough ideas based solely on their game profiles. Without ever meeting those 500 people or seeing their ideas, Knack's algorithm accurately pinpointed which of those employees had the best ideas. Now armed with that information, the game can be tuned to Shell's needs. In the future, workers who submit ideas will be evaluated on their performance in the game, allowing the company to quickly sift through the ideas to find the best ones.

Knack is now turning to campus recruiting, which Halfteck says is extremely outdated. Knack is working with colleges to open its games to students so they can demonstrate their skills to potential employers well before they ever hit the job market. Students earn badges as they play the games, such as Leadership, Grit, and Logistical Reasoning, which they can display online for potential employers to discover. These badges are like endorsements on LinkedIn, only these are verified by your game-playing abilities. Eventually, Halfteck expects the games to be used as a way to short-circuit the lengthy and ineffective recruitment process I explained earlier.

"The interview process will change its form and function," Halfteck said. "Instead of using the interview process to filter out the best candidates, you'll start the interview process with only the best candidates."

The ability to gather large amounts of data about a job candidate's skills opens up other ways to improve the hiring process. Right now, recruiting relies heavily on the exchange of information between employers and applicants. When companies determine they need to hire someone, they write a job description based on some abstract notion of their requirements, place an advertisement for the job, and then pray the right person sees the notice and applies. Job candidates submit documents they hope tell employers why they are qualified for the job. These documents are usually a diploma, transcript, and résumé that say little about what the students actually know, only that they made it successfully through four years of college and what they did while there.

Somehow after a few meetings, a match is made, but no one knows at the time if the applicant can actually do the job. Anyone who has ever done the hiring for a job has a story about a mistaken hire. According to one survey by the Corporate Executive Board, hiring managers regretted making offers to one in five people on their staff. That's a lot of bad matches.

Big data promises to transform the job hunt into a process of discovery, for both candidates and employers. One vision of the future has college students building online portfolios that demonstrate their skills and abilities with actual work samples attached. Instead of waiting for an application, employers will be able to search information that students make available online. This ability to discover applicants before they apply is already happening on sites like LinkedIn, where recruiters search online profiles to find candidates passively looking for a job.

The data on LinkedIn also provides college students with information on the paths people traveled to get their current jobs. The giant online professional networking site has more than 364 million members worldwide. It knows where most of its users went to college, their degrees, where they work, and what they do in those jobs. Indeed, it knows when people switch jobs before their alma mater does.

Since 2013, LinkedIn has been combing the details sprinkled throughout those profiles—skills, degrees, employers, occupations, and location—to build an array of new search tools to assist students in their hunt for a college and a career.

On a spring day in late March, I paid a visit to LinkedIn's sprawling headquarters campus in Mountain View, California, to find out what digital bread crumbs we all leave on the web could potentially remake how we think about choosing a major, a college, and eventually jobs and careers. The interrelated search engines LinkedIn has already built allow anyone to essentially reverse-engineer the career paths of members by navigating the connections between their majors, schools, and careers (you can find the search engines at linkedin.com/edu).

Say you want to know more about people who majored in biomedical engineering in college. The search on LinkedIn returns some sixty-six thousand LinkedIn members with that degree. Their top three employers: GE Healthcare, Medtronic, and Siemens Healthcare. Click on GE Healthcare to see that its nearly five hundred majors are employed as engineers, researchers, and in sales, and twenty of them went to Marquette University. Dive a little deeper into profiles to find out details about their lives, the jobs they held, their skill sets, and how they are connected to other companies and people.

Each click on LinkedIn essentially draws a picture of the

overlapping pathways people follow through their careers. If you want to be a history major in college and live in San Francisco after graduation, enter those terms, and LinkedIn spits out the colleges and universities where its databases contain the most people who studied history and work in the Bay Area: the University of California at Berkeley (Google is the biggest employer of its history graduates), San Francisco State (the biggest employer is Kaiser Permanente), and the University of California at Santa Cruz (the biggest employer is Apple). While only as accurate as the information embedded in the profiles, the results are nonetheless addictive if you're interested in what people ended up doing with their English literature degree or where they worked before they landed a great job at Google.

LinkedIn has ambitious plans to continue mining the data among its users to build what it calls the "economic graph," a real-time picture of employer needs and the skills people have around the world so that the two sides can more easily find each other.

Whether that happens or not, colleges and their job-seeking students already find the tools LinkedIn offers are helpful in connecting them with employers. The University of California at San Diego, for instance, witnessed a fivefold increase in the number of alumni it had employment information about after it partnered with LinkedIn to search through public profiles. The university discovered several alumni who worked in influential positions at Visa. It paid them a visit, and the company now sends recruiters to the university. In 2014, Visa hired twenty graduates. The number of graduates the company had hired in the previous five years combined? None.

The End for College Career Centers?

SOON AFTER THE WHARTON PEOPLE ANALYTICS CONFER-
ence, I attended a career fair at George Mason University,
a public institution with thirty-three thousand students in
the suburbs of Washington, D.C. That spring, the university
would graduate students into a job market that Phil Gardner
described as brutal. The pipeline to jobs is seriously clogged,
he said, as baby boomers are continuing to work well past the
traditional retirement age. One survey by Wells Fargo found
that 37 percent of boomers plan to work into their eighties.

The career fair was typical of one at basically any college
or university these days. Employers large and small, local and
international brands, set up tables around a large banquet
hall in the student center. Each table had a display touting
the benefits of working at Company X as a recruiter or two
stood in front, hoping to engage students in a conversation as
they wandered by. A few students were dressed in suits with
portfolios tucked under their arms, while others looked like
they had just rolled out of bed.

Whenever students and recruiters connected, the conversations were cursory and brief. No one would actually
get a job here. What the students heard about the available
jobs and the skills needed for each one was something they
should have heard four years earlier—which made this all
seem to be way too late.

I headed off to hear a presentation by a Google employee
named Brian, who had graduated a few years earlier with a
master's degree from George Mason. About two dozen stu-

dents showed up. Brian walked them through the perks of working at Google. Then he got into what everyone wanted to know: How exactly do you get a job at Google? His advice was simple: figure out a way to stand out. A freshman in the room asked how he should do that. "Write code, lots of it," Brian said.

Then he continued with a lengthy list of people he knew who got a job at Google and what they did: publish a paper, get a patent, present at a conference, or contribute to an open-source software project. His list surprised me, given that he was talking to a bunch of undergraduates, but not as much as it didn't seem to surprise them. Perhaps they didn't understand what was involved in accomplishing all that Brian enumerated. Then a senior asked if going to graduate school would make him stand out.

"Google doesn't care about your degrees, they care about what you know," Brian said, seemingly unaware for a moment that he was speaking at a place where the entire business model was built on selling degrees for tens of thousands of dollars to willing customers. "I could have gotten this job out of high school. I'm now shocked at how easy getting the bachelor's and master's degree was compared to what I'm doing."

In response to the growing concern that parents and students have about the return on their enormous investment in a bachelor's degree, colleges are slowly beginning to pay attention to their career services. In the last five years, nearly half of colleges and universities have increased the budget of their career offices, according to one survey.

Still, Andy Chan, vice president for personal and career development at Wake Forest University, estimates that two-thirds of the center directors he interacts with on a regular basis either come from institutions where top leaders and faculty care little about career services or don't think about it at all.

Chan is a rock star in the field. He has raised millions of dollars to expand Wake Forest's career services and has been featured in the *New York Times Magazine* for setting an example of what a career center should be in the twenty-first-century job market. Chan believes that personal interactions between college students and employers will continue to be a hallmark of the recruiting process.

"People hire people; they don't hire pieces of paper," he said.

But at the same time, Chan believes technology will play a larger role in personalizing the hiring process for college students. Today they live on their mobile devices, and they expect services on demand. Also, not all students are in the same place career-wise even if they are in similar spots in school.

Wake Forest used to target its services to specific class years. But then Chan realized that some freshmen were more advanced in their job search than some seniors. What's more, students in different majors approach the job search differently, just as companies in different industries recruit in different ways. So Wake Forest is beginning to abandon its one-size-fits-all approach and experimenting with a new technology platform called Handshake, which uses algorithms based on a student's profile to suggest pertinent information about recruiting and delivers alerts about campus career events to students' mobile phones.

"The next frontier is about personalizing and tailoring career information to students interests and needs," Chan told me.

When I first heard about people analytics matching students with jobs, I had the same worries I had when I heard about colleges using advanced algorithms to steer undergraduates to specific courses and majors. But the more time I spent observing the recruiting process for college seniors and interviewing young adults struggling to find jobs or their way in life, I began to see how people analytics could bring order to an often chaotic process and shine light into that black box of job matching to make it fairer for everyone. Because of its use of people analytics, Laszlo Bock at Google told me the company has increased the number of people it hires who don't have a college degree because that credential no longer ensures that someone is job ready.

But few believe that people analytics will eliminate the need for some form of college education. Education after high school will remain critically important to success in this economy and to the future of a democracy, but too many students blindly follow the path to college without knowing exactly what they want to get out of it, and once they are there, they don't make the right decisions to ensure that it pays off as a long-term investment.

Guided by algorithms—but not solely directed by them— students can begin to measure and showcase their natural talents as teenagers and achieve a better match to careers later in life, with or without finding the traditional on-ramp to college, and build their professional narrative for decades to come.

CHAPTER 10

TELLING YOUR CAREER STORY

Humans love stories—on the page, on the stage, and on the big screen. We like to empathize with characters, and we binge-watch television series with plots that twist and turn and advance at a gripping pace. I have described the journeys of young adults in this book not only so readers could identify with some of them, but also to illustrate the significance of starting to craft your own career narrative.

I've spent a lot of time with students and recruiters, managers and new graduates and other twentysomethings, and one line of questioning most often tripped them up: they could not easily tell their story of how they got to where they were in their lives.

Why did you major in X? How did you choose Y University? What motivated you to pursue the internship at Z company?

The particular questions you'll be asked differ depending

on your field and the job, but they all require responses that exhibit the soft skills employers are looking for: tolerance for ambiguity, experience with failure, and the willingness to learn.

Disney CEO Bob Iger said that in interviews he tries to prompt job candidates to craft their career stories and asks questions that will gauge their level of curiosity—the books they have read, the movies they have seen, or where they have recently traveled. Yet this strong narrative was what the recent college graduates I met at the Koru bridge program struggled with most. And it was the storytelling class at General Assembly that drove Allyson to improve her own elevator pitch for potential employers. People with good stories show employers they can transfer their learning from one environment to another, typically from the classroom to the workplace.

Lauren A. Rivera devoted an entire chapter in her book *Pedigree: How Elite Students Get Elite Jobs* to the importance of the candidate's narrative. For the employers she observed, "a good story provided a concise yet compelling abstract of the candidate's journey to the interview room—the social, educational, and occupational path the applicant had taken to reach this particular career juncture." According to Rivera, the interviewers "plumbed the person's story of the past to acquire a sense of his or her underlying drive."

This final chapter is meant to provide a cheat sheet to the major questions you should answer as you craft a career story:

What do my work and study experiences in college say about me? Do they reveal my core interests and passions?

What kind of working environments do I enjoy and do well in?

What failures did I experience in college, and what lessons did I learn from them?

What kind of job would give me a sense of fulfillment?

Where do I want to be in five years?

It's never too early to begin building your narrative, and it's never too late to write a new chapter, even if you consider yourself among the Stragglers. Shaping a career narrative is like building your own brand, and you need to be able to sell it to potential employers (or to investors, if you're an entrepreneur). Not only must you be an ideal candidate— you have to show them that you are.

Getting a job is a sales job. That's the advice I heard from Donn Davis, who runs a venture capital investment firm called Revolution along with two well-known pioneers of the Internet age: Steve Case, one of the founders of AOL, and Ted Leonsis, who now owns three of Washington's professional sports teams.

Revolution has made successful bets on start-up companies from the car-sharing service Zipcar to the deal site LivingSocial. So Davis has a lot of experience listening to pitches from entrepreneurs. He also teaches a long-running undergraduate class at his alma mater, Miami University in Ohio, called "Real Business." I met Davis in his office one morning, and he handed me a small laminated card that listed his ten simple rules of business. He gives the card to all the students in his course. Number five: Everything is sales.

He says it's the one rule his students too often fail to grasp about their own careers, and it's the one he also notices interns and young employees at his firm wrestle with in their day-to-day work.

Like it or not, we are all in sales today. According to author Daniel Pink, 40 percent of our work time is spent selling something—not just products, but trying to persuade, negotiate, and pitch ideas and techniques. Today's young adults struggle with selling themselves to get a job or, once they have one, struggle again with selling a concept or an opinion, because often they were never forced to justify their point of view or navigate their own lives until they graduated from college. Much is expected of twentysomethings these days, but they haven't been armed with the necessary coping skills for a job—learning to navigate workplace politics and to work with others, and getting support from their peers.

The emphasis schools place on science, technology, engineering, and math as well as standardized testing and rote memorization may teach students the logical and technical skills they need to do a job, but the college experience often fails to provide them with the necessary street smarts to apply those skills in whatever situation they may encounter. That capacity for developing and discovering new ideas is often provided by other academic disciplines, such as history, philosophy, or sociology. This is how we create the next Steve Jobs or Steven Spielberg and why a broad education should still matter to you, even though you might not understand that when you're eighteen years old. A good liberal arts education *combined with* a skills-based vocational education provides the "connective tissue" between disparate ideas and will help you navigate the ambiguous work world you are going to live in, where job requirements seem to change nearly every day and careers disappear with regularity.

What Employers Want to See in Your Story

YOUR STORY NEEDS TO BE AUTHENTIC AND TRUE. AND you should worry more about it being coherent than artful. Employers are looking for the *why* behind your decisions and *how* the situations you faced before might compare with ones you will confront on the job. To employers, the why shows intent and drive. It also shows them that you are able to connect the dots between your experiences. How did one internship you had lead to another? Why did you decide to take a detour by going on a gap year or even reverse course by changing majors? Why did you stay in that job for less than one year?

As I talked with Davis at Revolution, I noticed a collection of small glass boxes on the coffee table in front of him. Each one contained a business card from his career: general counsel for the Chicago Cubs; founder and president of Tribune Ventures; COO of Interactive Properties Group at AOL. They were signposts for his own career narrative, each one a chapter in an evolving story.

Figure out how to identify and leverage your own signposts. For college students, these signposts might not be jobs but courses, activities, or life-altering experiences. Find inspiration for your own story in the lives of others who have traveled the road before you. College offers plenty of opportunities to network with alumni who had the same major. Internships and part-time jobs land you in situations where you will work with people of various generations who are already doing the jobs you might want someday. In such circumstances, instead of asking alumni or coworkers for routine career advice, ask them to tell you their stories. People love to talk about how they got to where they are today. In doing so, you will get the advice you were initially seeking but will also hear how they construct their narratives. Listen for how they make the connections between what they learned and where they learned it, and ultimately how they applied their learning in different jobs.

Reading or hearing someone else's career narrative is instructive, but remember you need to write your own. Don't live someone else's ambitions for your life (and that includes those of your parents). Building your career narrative is relevant whether you are a senior in high school, a senior in college, or even a few years out from your undergraduate experience. Here are three important questions to consider as you write your story.

What Do I Want to Do When I Grow Up?

Ask anyone working today if they knew exactly what they wanted to do with their lives at age eighteen, and they will probably say they had no idea (if they're being honest). The longer they have been in the workforce, the less likely it is that they are in a career directly related to their college major. Yet today, for some reason, we expect teenagers to know exactly what they're going to do in the workforce of the future.

After "Where are you going to college?" the second most-asked question of every high school graduate is "What do you plan to study?" Better follow-ups (and for the graduates to ask themselves) would be "Why did you choose that school?" or "What are you hoping to accomplish there?" It's no wonder that eighteen-year-olds get anxious over choosing a major.

Does a college major matter to success in one's career? It depends on whom you ask and what goals you have for your career.

If money is your goal, Tony Carnevale at Georgetown University's Center on Education and the Workforce will tell you that a certain group of majors provide a bigger return on investment over a lifetime. He has found that of the twenty-five highest-paying majors, all but two (economics and business economics) are in STEM fields. Even so, Carnevale warns students who pick their majors solely on the basis of the expected paycheck not to count their money too quickly. Salaries for specific majors can differ greatly, too. The top quarter earners who majored in humanities or the liberal arts make more than the bottom quarter of engineering majors. What's more, only 22 percent of graduates with degrees in science and math actually get jobs in those fields and utilize their training.

If career advancement is your goal, some majors do a much better job than others at graduating students with more of the reasoning skills sought by employers in today's workplace. As I mentioned earlier, results of national tests and several recent studies have shown that students who major in mathematics, science, and engineering, as well as the traditional liberal arts (philosophy, history, and literature), make larger gains in learning complex skills than do those who study business or service fields, such as social work and education. Ultimately, how hard you work in your classes directly affects how much you learn and eventually how well you launch after graduation.

One more study to add to this mix comes from the Brookings Institution in Washington, D.C., which analyzed the market value of the twenty-five most commonly cited skills listed by alumni of each college in their LinkedIn profiles. What it demonstrated was that skill development, not your undergraduate major or the college you choose, is most critical to your earnings potential.

Picking a major is not like buying a new car, however. You can't easily test-drive a major (unless you plan to stay in college for many more than four years) or compare them beyond the data Georgetown publishes on earnings. A major reflects your interests at one moment in your life. Where you end up in a career is the result of a meandering pathway that most college graduates are destined to take after graduation. Some graduates apply their majors to their careers more than others, and some not at all.

I was reminded of the tenuous connection between college majors and careers when I went to the Declaration Dinner at Franklin & Marshall College, a small liberal arts school in Lancaster, Pennsylvania. Students at F&M don't need to officially declare a major until the end of their sophomore year. At this annual dinner, students sit at tables grouped by their newly declared major and with that department's faculty members and alumni who graduated with the degree.

At the philosophy table, I sat next to Katelyn Greller. She

told me her major often elicits questions from adults who wonder what she's going to do with the degree. "I don't know yet," she said. "But it will give me a good foundation in reading, writing, and critical thinking, and that will prove useful in many fields." She already had a good start to her career narrative. Nearby, Richard Bidgood, who graduated from F&M in 1976 with a philosophy degree, agreed. He had recently retired from banking, a field that tends to attract finance, business, and economics majors. He said his colleagues appreciated his philosophy background. "It helped me think through problems when we were making deals and ask the right questions," he said.

F&M's president, Dan Porterfield, told the students that choosing a major is a "statement of interest, value, and identity." He reminded them that some of the college's most successful alumni majored in something unrelated to their current career field. Mary Schapiro, the former chair of the U.S. Securities and Exchange Commission, received her degree in anthropology. Richard Plepler, president of HBO, majored in government.

Colleges like having majors because it is an efficient way to organize faculty members by departments. But that doesn't mean students need to organize themselves in the same way. The project to rethink undergraduate education at Stanford that I wrote about in Chapter 8 suggested that in the future, instead of declaring majors, students would declare a "mission" to help them find meaning and purpose in their studies. Students today are commonly told they should follow their passions and find a mission in life, but very few eighteen-year-olds or even twenty-two-year-olds have enough experience in the world to know what truly excites them. Pick a major that interests you, but allow it and external experiences to help shape, not dictate, your mission in life.

While you should consider different majors, and you should keep your options open for a while, don't think you can do anything you want or have all the time in the world to make a decision. Talent and drive matters to success in most majors, of course. You can't major in physics if you're terrible at math. And at some point, you need to focus on a major (or maybe two) because organizations want workers who are grounded in at least one discipline—the vertical line of the T-shaped person—not employees who dart around without ever developing a specific skill set.

Everywhere I go, parents and students ask me for advice about choosing a major. Here's what I tell them: find a major that will challenge you to work hard and one that will present you with opportunities to learn from the best professors and mentors. You might need to spend two semesters exploring and wait until the end of your freshman year to declare a major. That's okay because you'll still have time to line up the internships and other experiences to sprint out of college. Avoid majors that are narrow in their focus or that seem to appeal to the latest job trends, unless they are focused on fixing things (engineers, welders, electricians) or fixing people (nurses, physical therapists).

No one can predict what the job market will look like in two or four years, yet that's the pitch you will hear from most colleges with vocational majors: they'll get you a job. Sure, such majors will teach you the specific skills and language of an industry, but you can learn that in the real world during internships or co-ops. What you won't get in the workplace are the critical thinking, writing, and communications skills that come from the liberal arts (and I'm including the hard sciences in that category).

Finally, if you're unsure about what you want to do after high school or even once you get to college, take a gap year or time off and explore life in the real world outside of the artificial environment that is college. The biggest problem with young adults struggling to launch is that they haven't seen most jobs up close so the options are overwhelming to them. Higher education is too expensive to wander through it without any sort of plan or goals.

The results of my own survey show that if you're unsure of your major or change it several times, you're more likely to wander through your twenties. Time off will allow you to see real jobs in action and arm you with the knowledge and maturity needed to make better decisions about what you're going to do with your life.

Where to Start My Education and My Career?

Every spring, when college acceptance letters roll in for high school seniors, much of the national media's focus is on a select group of students vying to get into the country's three dozen or so most selective colleges and universities. Stanford, Harvard, Princeton, and others brag in press releases that they accepted only one out of every ten applicants, setting another record for how many students they rejected, including hundreds of high school valedictorians.

But for all the attention showered on these elite colleges and universities, they enroll less than 6 percent of U.S. college students. Yet for a variety of reasons—reputation, peer and parental pressure—students feel compelled to pursue these "brass ring" institutions. Students, parents, and counselors can reduce anxiety and frustration if instead they would focus on *why* students should go to college more than the name. Although college makes sense for most, college isn't only a four-year residential experience that starts three months after high school graduation. That's what "college" might mean to your parents or guidance counselors, but there are plenty of good community colleges and apprenticeships to further your education that often lead to better jobs than you would get with a bachelor's degree.

What you do in school is more important than where you go. But there are times when it does matter where you go to school.

For one, the amount of student loan debt you have at graduation has a direct impact on the choices you'll make in the years immediately after college. Debt determines your ability to move for a job, the salary you'll need to earn, and the possibility you can strike out on your own as an entrepreneur. According to my own survey for this book, 43 percent of Sprinters had less than $10,000 of loan debt. There is no perfect rule for how much debt is too much, but be sure you're not above the national average ($30,000) or in debt for more than the typical starting salary for a bachelor's degree ($39,000).

You should also consider the graduation rate for students similar to you, which can differ by gender, major, and family background. Check them out and compare colleges. The peer effects of an undergraduate education are critical to your ultimate success in the workplace—your fellow students can push you to study harder and help you find many of the best internship and job opportunities down the road. You want to go to a school with students as interested in obtaining an education and a credential as you are, and not those simply looking for a place to hang out for a few years.

Resist the urge to simply follow the prestige of the various rankings. Go to a place where you'll learn *and* do, such as the campuses mentioned throughout the book—Northeastern and Cincinnati, which offer the co-op experience; community colleges with their workforce programs; Arizona State with its new project-based degree; or the University of Southern California and American University, where being in a dynamic city is part of your education. I'm a fan of the intimacy of learning at the small liberal arts colleges mentioned in the book, too, but if you go that route, be sure that you find the outside-the-classroom experiences that are so critical to success.

For all the time and attention students and their families place on the college search, they spend comparatively little on the search for the right job a few years later. Given the current state of the job market, you might not have many choices. But don't take *any* job to say you have one at graduation. Jobs that recent graduates took only to "pay the bills" often put them in the category of the underemployed. I met many Wanderers who still had those first jobs a few years after commencement and were now competing with a new crop of graduates as their own skills degraded with each passing year. Indeed, in my survey, Sprinters were twice as likely as everyone else to be employed within six months after graduation, nearly all of them in jobs related to their major.

Meanwhile, only half of the Wanderers were employed—and of those who were working, 85 percent were in jobs unrelated to their major. The bottom line is to make every attempt you can to find a job in the field you want to work in, even if you have to move or take a smaller salary to do so. And if you feel as if you're in the wrong job, take time to reassess your plans and perhaps gain new skills by going back to school, heading off to a boot camp, or finding free online courses. There's no reason to stay on a particular road if you feel it's taking you in the wrong direction. This is your time to take risks and learn to navigate the workplace you're going to live in for the next thirty-plus years.

When you have a choice, go to an employer that is growing or where you'll learn on the job, not someplace where you'll just be a number with few opportunities for advancement or professional development. To succeed in this economy, you'll need to constantly sharpen your skills throughout your career. You might as well do that on the job or you will need to pay for it yourself somewhere else. It's also okay to switch employers often in your twenties. Adults who have a multitude of obligations probably will tell you otherwise, but the research shows that the twenties are when young adults set up for success later in life and determine how much they eventually earn and the positions they hold. When you're an undergraduate, take the job hunt as seriously as you did the search for a college, because where you work after graduation might matter more in the long run than where you went to school.

How to Thrive in My Career?

As a journalist covering higher education, I often see studies about the value of college as well as rankings that purport to tell students which schools are the best for them. One that caught my attention was from Gallup and Purdue University about the pathways young adults take to make "great lives" and have "great jobs." The Gallup-Purdue poll surveyed some 30,000 bachelor's degree recipients and 1,500 associate's degree holders nationwide to measure their well-being (that is, being happy, comfortable, and satisfied) in five dimensions: social, financial, sense of purpose, connectedness to their community, and physical health. Only 11 percent of college graduates are thriving in all five dimensions. More than one in six aren't thriving in any.

The survey found that well-being has less to do with where you go to college and more with what you do while you are there. College graduates who said they had a professor who cared about them as a person and encouraged them to follow their dreams were more than twice as likely to be engaged in life and work after graduation—meaning they were curious, interested, and had a passion for what they were doing. The same was true for graduates with outside-the-classroom experiences, internships, research projects, campus clubs, and athletic teams. But here's the problem: only 14 percent of graduates recalled having a professor who made them excited about learning and encouraged them.

The Gallup-Purdue poll also looked at how engaged workers are on the job. According to the survey, 39 percent of college graduates are engaged in their job, compared with

30 percent of the U.S. population overall. While a spread of 9 percentage points might not sound like much, Brandon Busteed, executive director of Gallup Education, described it as significant.

Although more male college graduates than female graduates are employed full-time, women with a college degree are more engaged in their work than men. And here was another survey that found differences among college majors. Science and business majors are more likely to be employed full-time than other majors, but those who majored in the arts and humanities are more engaged in their work than anyone else.

To thrive in your career, don't treat college or your job as a spectator sport. Colleges have added computerized advising systems and human advisers in recent years, but neither of them gives students the advice they really need. Recall the seniors at Oregon State from Chapter 1 who said no one told them to visit their professors for advice during office hours. Find professors and mentors in the workplace who will guide you on your journey. Begin to build your professional network in college, in your internships, and in your first jobs.

Develop the soft skills described in Chapter 2 that employers increasingly seek. These skills will help ensure you'll remain employed as automation threatens more jobs. Focus on two skills in particular once in the job. One: remain curious and always seek out opportunities to learn. Knowledge workers need to stay one step ahead of intelligent machines by moving to even higher levels of cognition or specializing in areas not yet automatized or ones humans don't want robots to do.

Second: follow the advice of Mary Egan, formerly of Star-bucks, who now has her own start-up in Seattle. If you are a new employee "climb the ladder of leverage" in an organi-zation by doing more of what's on your boss's or coworkers' plates. You'll not only learn new things, but will become more valuable to your employer.

A few years after I met the two young alumni from David-son College during my trip on the Millennial Trains Proj-ect, Davidson's president, Carol Quillen, invited me to the North Carolina campus for a visit. Like higher education leaders across the country, Quillen was grappling with the issue of job readiness for her young graduates.

Soon after she took over at Davidson, Quillen had vis-ited New York City, where she had dinner with a group of successful alumni who told her that Davidson graduates make good hires, but not right out of school. They need more seasoning, she was told. Quillen was trying to figure out how Davidson could provide that finishing experience without adding time or expense to an already overstretched bachelor's degree.

"Students need more exposure to the real world of work," said Quillen, a scholar of Italian humanism by training. "The rules have changed."

Students and their parents expect an immediate payoff for their degree given its cost. With wages falling for those who have recently earned bachelor's degrees, American higher education risks irrelevance if its institutions continue to edu-cate students for a world that no longer exists.

Quillen is one of a few college presidents who understands

that something significant is happening in the economy, and in recent years, she has created a series of paid fellowships and academic programs at Davidson to help students better translate their liberal arts training into the work world, an effort she calls "transition to impact."

I arrived at Davidson late on a spring afternoon and was given the requisite campus tour. My guide was named Anna, a senior economics major who was a month away from graduation. She had arrived at Davidson with plans to go to medical school, but after graduation would take a job as a business consultant in nearby Charlotte, an offer she received after an internship the previous summer. Now she was giving tours to high school seniors who had been accepted to Davidson and probably several other top schools. They were making their decisions about where to spend the next four years. I asked her what advice she gave them.

"Davidson is not going to hold your hand for four years. Your undergraduate career is open-ended and uncertain. Advisers are not going to tell you what classes to take and professors are not going to tell you what to write in a paper or which internships to apply for. You need to develop the ability to manage your life, complete tasks, and try to reach your own goals."

For a moment, I wondered if this was also advice Anna was giving to her future self—she would need to make her own way in a career as she had done in college. She had recognized when she arrived at Davidson that despite the mystique surrounding the bachelor's degree, it alone wasn't enough to provide her with a good job after graduation. She needed to actively manage her own undergraduate career by learning *and* doing. Now she would need to employ the same approach through her first decade in the workplace, a period that Georgetown's Tony Carnevale calls the "learning and earning" stage of life.

For previous generations, the job after college often led to lifetime employment and advancement in one company, but today's rocky job market requires not only getting off to the right start, but also continuing to navigate your own learning throughout life.

The twenty-first-century economy demands a higher level of talent who practice both classroom learning and hands-on learning in tandem. If you are to thrive in this new economy, you must resist the temptation of the protective bubble that colleges increasingly provide you. Rather, you need to navigate a career that promises many more twists and turns as technology continues to automate and replace jobs.

Throughout much of human history, the answer to staying ahead of automation was more education. That's still the case, but now the answer is much more ambiguous and complicated. Just going to college will not land you meaningful employment. The biggest employers of tomorrow will be able to get by with far fewer workers. The challenge to young adults today is to stand out in this competitive economy with a career story that resonates with employers. To succeed you will have to learn to manage the many pathways available to find the right kinds of educational opportunities, at the right time, to achieve the life you desire.

APPENDIX: SURVEY RESULTS

Young adults in their twenties make up about one-third of the U.S. population. They are now the biggest generation in the workforce. In the nearly two years I spent researching and writing this book, I met dozens of twentysomethings who were at different stages in starting their careers. How and when they launched differed substantially, with some of them taking most of their twenties to find their way in life. For many, a college credential alone wasn't the ticket to a good life and a good job as it had been for so many of their counterparts in previous generations.

I wanted to know more about their experiences as students—did their choice of school or major or how much loan debt they had at graduation impact how they started in their career? To find the answer to that question and others, I commissioned a survey with Maguire Associates, a higher education consulting firm outside of Boston that works with admissions offices and frequently polls students on what they think about colleges.

We conducted a survey of young adults who had at least some college experience and were born between 1988 and 1991. We chose those years so that we could capture people partway through their twenties who'd had some time to start a career. The ten-minute, twenty-three-question online survey was completed by 752 people in early August 2015.* For privacy reasons, we didn't collect identifying information about the participants beyond basic demographic details.

Overview

WHEN I ANALYZED THE RESULTS, I DISCOVERED BROAD trends that allowed me to divide the respondents into the three primary clusters defined in Chapter 1: Sprinters, Wanderers, and Stragglers. There were some subtle differences within two of the groups—Wanderers and Stragglers—so I divided those clusters into the subcategories described below. The three primary groups were fairly evenly divided, with each making up about one-third of respondents.

---

* We invited members of a nationally representative research panel recruited and managed by Qualtrics.

Sprinters

Sprinters are twentysomethings who either get a fast start in their career or who are on a path to a successful launch after completing additional education. This group comprised 35 percent of survey respondents. In general, they come from families with college-educated parents, have low levels of student loan debt, are sure of their major early in their undergraduate career, have at least one internship in college, and find a full-time job within six months after graduation.

Key Markers of a Sprinter

79% have at least one internship while in college

64% are sure of their major when they begin college

50% have college-educated parents

43% have less than $10,000 in student loan debt

30% study a STEM (science, technology, engineering, and math) field

Wanderers

Wanderers take about half their twenties to get their start in a career. Overall, Wanderers made up 32 percent of respondents. There are two types of Wanderers, according to the survey. The larger of the two subgroups, the Determined Wanderers, accounted for 22 percent of respondents, with the smaller subgroup, the Wavering Wanderers, making up the rest at 10 percent.

In general, Wanderers attend a public four-year institution, are less certain of their major when they enter college, and do not find work right after school or, if they do, work in a job unrelated to their major. Women make up a much larger proportion of Wanderers than do men largely because they outnumber men in college enrollment. Men who would likely become Wanderers don't go to college at all and then fall into the third group, the Stragglers.

Key Markers of a Determined Wanderer

85% begin working in a job unrelated to their college major

66% are women

58% are less than certain of their major when entering college

53% don't find work immediately after college

51% first attended a public four-year college

Key Markers of a Wavering Wanderer

95% don't find work immediately after college

76% have not yet landed their first job

51% do not pursue internships in college

28% do not have a college-educated parent

Stragglers

Stragglers take nearly all of their twenties to get their start in a career. Overall, Stragglers made up 33 percent of respondents. There are two types of Stragglers, according to the survey. One group of Stragglers tends to be closely related to the Wanderers. They are the Persevering Stragglers, who made up 13 percent of respondents. The remaining twenty-somethings were Idle Stragglers, who accounted for 22 percent of respondents.

In general, Stragglers attend public institutions (both two- and four-year schools) and go to school part-time. Many times they end up not graduating and then frequently change jobs once they are in a career.

Key Markers of a Persevering Straggler

70% are part-time students

63% are not certain of their major when entering college

52% attend a two-year institution

37% take time off after high school for a nonacademic reason (not for a gap year, but for financial or family circumstances)

Key Markers of an Idle Straggler

77% do not pursue internships in college

55% are not certain of their major when entering college

54% fail to find work immediately after college

How to Get Off to the Right Start
in a Career

HOW YOUNG ADULTS START THEIR CAREERS IS LARGELY A result of their choices during their undergraduate studies, according to the survey.

What can you do to ensure that you successfully launch your work life?

Based on the results of the survey, your best bet is to choose a major early on in school and then line up the appropriate internships and work experiences throughout your undergraduate career. Students who switch majors often or took a long time to settle on a major and then didn't have any internships in college struggled in settling into a career.

STEM majors turn into Sprinters more often than students who majored in other fields, according to the survey. That's often the case because there is demand for top graduates in those programs. But the popularity of your major doesn't guarantee success in the job market. Business majors, the most popular undergraduate major, are a significant part of every cluster in the survey from Sprinters to Stragglers.

What role does your college play in how you start off? I didn't gather enough details about the institutions from which survey respondents graduated to draw any specific conclusions on this question. But there has been a slew of academic research on this topic, much of it with inconclusive and sometimes contradictory findings. The research seems to indicate that how engaged you are in your undergraduate studies matters more to your ultimate success than where you go to school. In other words, even graduates of Harvard struggle in the job market.

But as I said, the research is at times contradictory. Scholars have found evidence that where you go to school might have an impact on how you at least get *started* in your career. In the 2014 book *Aspiring Adults Adrift,* the authors followed 1,600 students who made the transition from college to the workforce or graduate school. They found students who went to selective colleges made larger gains on a national test of general collegiate skills between their freshman and senior years of college. After they graduated, students with high scores had low levels of unemployment and underemployment.

Selective schools are not just the Ivy League and some small private liberal arts colleges. When researchers study selective colleges, they usually mean a group of 200 to 250 institutions, both public and private, based on categories chosen by Barron's, which publishes a popular college guide. The list includes a diverse set of institutions including the College of New Jersey, State University of New York at Binghamton, and Ohio State.

It's unclear why a school's selectivity seems to matter early in a graduate's career but not as much later on. One explanation is that students who go to selective schools tend to graduate at higher rates than at less selective institutions and they build a network of peers who go on to good jobs. The usefulness of that collegiate network might dissipate over time as people spend more time in the job market and build their own networks independent of their undergraduate alma mater.

ACKNOWLEDGMENTS

FIRST AND FOREMOST, MY WIFE, HEATHER SALKO, HAS BEEN A CONSTANT SOURCE OF LOVE AND ENCOURAGEMENT SINCE WE MET FIFTEEN YEARS AGO. After I wrote my first book, I pledged to never do another one. I think she believed me. Her patience and support during the many late nights and weekends I spent writing made this endeavor possible with two young children at home.

To my daughters, Hadley and Rory, who will never know how much they inspired the many stories throughout this book by their endless curiosity. I hope you never lose that desire to always learn. I love you more than words can adequately describe on any page.

My parents, Jim and Carmella; my sister, Jamie; and my brother, Dave, have always been there for me, to guide me, help me, and support me no matter which route I decided to take through life. My in-laws, Gene and Sandy Salko, were generous with their time as always, willing to drop anything to help out. I could not do what I do without Maria Orozco. Thanks to her, I never worry about my daughters when my wife and I are not around.

Plenty of people and organizations are responsible for helping me during the year and a half I researched and wrote this book, starting with those who supported me in my day-to-day work.

I'm grateful to Josh White and Marty Baron at the *Washington Post* for bringing me on as a contributor to their new higher ed venture, *Grade Point,* and allowing me to test out ideas for this book and reprint some of my posts here. Also a big thanks to Michael Crow, president of Arizona State University, and Jim O'Brien for giving me a perch as a professor of practice and special adviser to continue to watch the evolution of higher education; and to Rich DeMillo at the Georgia Institute of Technology for inspiring me with his own writing about the future of higher education and taking me on as a visiting scholar at Georgia Tech's Center for 21st Century Universities.

I owe special gratitude to the *Chronicle of Higher Education,* where I first started writing about higher education in 1997 and where parts of this book first appeared in one form or another as I became a part-time contributor in recent years. I'm thankful to the *Chronicle*'s editor, Liz McMillen, and its editor in chief, Michael Riley, for their permission to reprint some of my reporting in this book.

My agent, Gail Ross, persuaded me that my ideas were ripe enough to start researching, and she helped me shape a proposal and then communicate its vision in a way I wasn't able to in the very early days of this project. I owe her a tremendous debt for leading me to my editor, Henry Ferris.

His interest in this topic as a parent of college-age children turned a manuscript into a book that others in his situation would want to read. Thanks to Henry and his colleagues, including Nick Amphlett, at HarperCollins and its William Morrow imprint for their enthusiasm in shepherding this book to publication.

A number of people generously gave of their time to help me understand the changing nature of the job search for today's college graduates, but none more than Patricia Rose at the University of Pennsylvania, who also made several important introductions to corporate recruiters.

Jack Maguire has been a friend as long as he's been a source of keen insight and knowledge about the complex world of college admissions, and I thank him and his colleagues at Maguire Associates, including Ismael Carreras, Sarah Enterline, and Jim Murtha, for agreeing to take on the immense task (and cost) of the survey of twentysomethings used throughout this book. Two researchers, Meg Handley and Renata Opoczynski, helped me track down sources and find statistics, but any errors of fact or interpretation are mine alone.

Sheila McMillen and Katie Salisbury had the patience to read early drafts of the manuscript several times and were never shy about pointing out all the parts that didn't quite work or needed additional reporting.

A number of other people read selected chapters, provided feedback, and helped me think about the book's overall structure and how best to tell this complicated tale to a wide audience. Goldie Blumenstyk, Mitch Gerber, Paul Heaton, Dan Porterfield, Matt Reed, Tracey Selingo, and Martin VanDerWerf all had a hand in improving this book. Many of them also were there to listen to me talk about the book almost ad nauseam whenever I needed a break, a prerequisite it seems for anyone who knows an author. I especially want to thank Scott Smallwood, who I hired as my managing editor at *The Chronicle* many years ago and was an endless source of ideas about the structure and tone of this book. He remains one of the best editors I ever had the opportunity to work with in my career.

As I heard the career stories of dozens of people profiled in this book, I was often reminded of my own narrative and the people who helped me navigate the twists and turns of my career over the past twenty years, most of all in reporting and writing this book.

When I left for Ithaca College in the summer of 1991, I had my heart set on becoming a journalist, on seeing the world as a correspondent for a major television network. On the second day of classes, I met another freshman who had similar dreams, but who at the age of eighteen already had experience and the raw talent necessary to realize his goals.

It was an early lesson to have interests and passions, but also to be sure your expectations are grounded in the real world. College provides that reality check for young people through exploration. During that period in my own life, I came to appreciate my passion for journalism was better suited in writing for newspapers and magazines. It was a de-cision that led me down a route to wonderful places over the past two decades. And what happened to that other fresh-man? David Muir not only became a good friend, but on the day I sold this book idea he was named anchor of *ABC World News Tonight*.

As I mentioned throughout these pages, the impact of

your peers in the transition to a career cannot be overstated. Many of the people from my late teens and early twenties may no longer be part of my daily life, but they helped shape my education and my career to ensure that I started with a strong foundation of the soft skills necessary to succeed in life.

The lesson is that none of us gets to where we are on our own, and the same is true in writing a book.

NOTES

Introduction

x *bachelor's degree has declined 10 percent:* Jaison R. Abel, Richard Deitz, and Yaqin Su, "Are Recent College Graduates Finding Good Jobs?" *Current Issues in Economics and Finance* 20, no. 1 (2014), https://www.newyorkfed.org/medialibrary/media/research/current_issues/ci20-1.pdf.

x *report by three economists in 2014:* Paul Beaudry, David A. Green, and Benjamin M. Sand, "The Great Reversal in the Demand for Skill and Cognitive Tasks," NBER Working Paper No. 18901, National Bureau of Economic Research, Cambridge, MA, 2013.

xvi *until their thirtieth birthday:* Anthony P. Carnevale, Andrew P. Hanson, and Artem Gulish, *Failure to Launch: Structural Shift and the New Lost Generation,* Georgetown Center on Education and the Workforce, Washington, D.C., 2013.

xvii *One out of every three children:* Kaare Christensen, Gabriele Doblhammer, Roland Rau, and James W. Vaupel, "Ageing Populations: The Challenges Ahead," *Lancet* 374 (2009): 1196–208.

xviii *a study from Oxford University:* Carl Benedikt Frey and Michael A. Osborne, "The Future of Employment: How Susceptible Are Jobs to Computerisation?" Programme on the Impacts of Future Technology, Oxford Martin School, University of Oxford, September 17, 2013.

Chapter 1: The Sprinters, Wanderers, and Stragglers

1   *Stanley Hall grew up:* Details of Hall's life from Duane P. Schultz and Sydney Ellen Schultz, *A History of Modern Psychology,* 9th ed. (New York: Wadsworth, 2008), 199–205.

2   *"I am twenty-five":* Quoted in Ann Hulbert, *Raising America: Experts, Parents, and a Century of Advice About Children* (New York: Knopf, 2003), 55.

3   *Hall described this transitional period:* G. Stanley Hall, *Adolescence: Its Psychology and Its Relations to Physiology, Anthropology, Sociology, Sex, Crime, Religion, and Education,* 2 vols. (New York: D. Appleton, 1904).

4   *Between 1950 and 1960:* Elizabeth Fussell and Frank F. Furstenberg Jr., "The Transition to Adulthood During the Twentieth Century: Race, Nativity, and Gender," in *On the Frontier of Adulthood: Theory, Research, and Public Policy,* ed. Richard A. Settersten Jr., Frank F. Furstenberg Jr., and Rubén G. Rumbaut (Chicago: University of Chicago Press, 2005), 48–49.

5   *In 1970, factory work:* "Industrial Metamorphosis," *Economist,* September 29, 2005.

5   *The increase in the wage premium:* Jonathan James, "The College Wage Premium," *Economic Commentary,* Federal Reserve Bank of Cleveland, Number 2012-10, August 8, 2012.

7   *"Emerging adults often explore":* Jeffrey Jensen Arnett, "Emerging Adulthood: A Theory of Development from the Late Teens Through the Twenties," *American Psychologist* 55, no. 5 (May 2000): 469–80.

8   *Nearly 90 percent of those:* Jeffrey Jensen Arnett and Joseph Schwab, "Poll of Emerging Adults: Thriving, Struggling & Hopeful," survey, Clark University, Worcester, MA, December 2012.

8   *some 40 percent were unable:* Jeffrey Jensen Arnett and Joseph Schwab, "Becoming Established Adults: Busy, Joyful, Stressed—and Still Dreaming Big," survey, Clark University, Worcester, MA, October 2014.

11–12   *The average American holds eight different jobs:* Bureau of Labor Statistics, U.S. Department of Labor, "National Longitudinal Survey of Youth 1979," http://www.bls.gov/nls/nlsy79.htm.

12   *it takes four years to find a job:* Julie A. Yates, "The Transition from School to Work: Education and Work Experiences," *Monthly Labor Review,* February 2005.

13   *the average class of 2014 graduate:* Phil Izzo, "Congratulations to Class of 2014, Most Indebted Class Ever," *The Numbers* (blog), *Wall Street Journal,* May 16, 2014, http://blogs.wsj.com/numbers/congatulations-to-class-of-2014-the-most-indebted-ever-1368/.

13   *an extensive University of Arizona study:* Arizona Pathways to Life Success for University Students (APLUS), *Life After College: Drivers for Young Adult Success,* Norton School of Family and Consumer Sciences, University of Arizona, Tucson, June 2014.

13   *six in ten college students:* College Board, *Trends in Student Aid,* 2014.

14   *only 17 percent of twentysomethings:* Federal Reserve, *2013 Survey of Consumer Finances,* http://www.federalreserve.gov/econresdata/scf/scfindex.htm.

15   *Nearly 30 percent of recent graduates:* Richard Arum and Josipa Roksa, *Aspiring Adults Adrift: Tentative Transitions of College Graduates* (Chicago: University of Chicago Press, 2014).

17   *A quarter of all freshmen:* Cooperative Institutional Research Program, *The American Freshman: National Norms Fall 2014,* Higher Education Research Institute, University of California, Los Angeles, 2014; Cooperative Institutional Research Program, *Findings from the 2014 Administration of the Your First College Year (YFCY),* Higher Education Research Institute, University of California, Los Angeles, 2014.

17   *unable to land a full-time job:* National Association of Colleges and Employers, *First Destinations for the College Class of 2014,* Bethlehem, PA, May 2015, https://www.naceweb.org/uploadedFiles/Pages/surveys/first-destination/nace-first-destination-survey-final-report-05-2015.pdf.

18   *total student debt tripled:* APLUS, *Life After College.*

19   *three-quarters of their wage growth:* Richard Settersten and Barbara Ray, *Not Quite Adults: Why 20-Somethings Are Choosing a Slower Path to Adulthood, and Why It's Good for Everyone* (New York: Bantam Books, 2010), 73.

20   *"Graduates' first jobs":* Austan Goolsbee, "Hello, Young Workers: One Way to Reach the Top Is to Start There," *New York Times,* May 25, 2006.

22   *95 percent of high school seniors:* National Center for Educational Statistics, U.S. Department of Education, "National Educational Longitudinal Survey 1988"; Bureau of Labor Statistics, U.S. Department of Labor, "College Enrollment and Work Activity of 2014 High School Graduates," April 16, 2015, http://www.bls.gov/news.release/hsgec.nr0.htm.

23   *12.5 million twentysomethings:* National Student Clearinghouse Research Center, *Some College, No Degree: A National View of Students with Some College Enrollment, but No Completion,* July 2014, http://nscresearchcenter.org/signaturereport7/.

27   *College students in 1961:* Philip Babcock and Mindy Marks, "Leisure College, USA: The Decline in Student Study Time," *Education Outlook,* no. 7, American Enterprise Institute for Public Policy Research, Washington, D.C., August 2010.

Chapter 2: What the Economy Needs, What Employers Want

29   *the first Internet connection:* "IBM Research: Almaden," accessed April 19, 2015, http://www.research.ibm.com/labs/almaden/.

30   *a kind of Renaissance man:* David Guest, "The Hunt Is on for the Renaissance Man of Computing," *Independent* (London), September 17, 1991.

37   *ask their parents:* Po Bronson and Ashley Merryman, "The Creativity Crisis," *Newsweek,* July 10, 2010.

39   *a quarter of their week:* Richard Arum and Josipa Roksa, *Academically Adrift: Limited Learning on College Campuses* (Chicago: University of Chicago Press, 2011).

39   *"collegiate day of rest":* Katie Hafner, "How Thursday Became the New Friday," *New York Times,* November 6, 2005.

41   *production of movies, books, and video games:* Fareed Zakaria, *In Defense of a Liberal Education* (New York: W. W. Norton, 2015).

47   *The A is the most common grade:* Stuart Rojstaczer and Christopher Healy, "Where A Is Ordinary: The Evolution of American College and University Grading, 1940–2009," *Teachers College Record* 114, no. 7 (2012).

47   *certain fire in their belly:* Lauren A. Rivera, *Pedigree: How Elite Students Get Elite Jobs* (Princeton, NJ: Princeton University Press, 2015), 254.

50   *"the act of coding":* Marcus Wohlsen, "Digital Literacy Is the Key to the Future, but We Still Don't Know What It Means," *Wired,* September 15, 2014.

50   *1.4 million jobs:* Peg Tyre, "Is Coding the New Second Language?" *Smithsonian,* May 23, 2013.

53   *"go at it vigorously":* Quoted in David Glenn, "Carol Dweck's Attitude," *Chronicle of Higher Education,* May 9, 2010.

58   *Nearly all the chief academic officers:* Gallup/*Inside Higher Ed,* "Survey of College and University Chief Academic Officers," January 2014.

58   *11 percent of business leaders:* Gallup/Lumina Foundation, "U.S. Business Leaders Poll on Higher Education," *What America Needs to Know About Higher Education Redesign,* February 2014.

Chapter 3: The Benefits of a Detour

63   *less than half of high school graduates:* National Center for Education Statistics, U.S. Department of Education, "Digest of Education Statistics," table 302.10, 2014.

66   *The stereotype stems:* Joseph O'Shea, *Gap Year: How Delaying College Changes People in Ways the World Needs* (Baltimore, MD: Johns Hopkins University Press, 2013).

66   *estimated two hundred thousand students:* Eric Hoover, "More Students Decide That College Can Wait," *Chronicle of Higher Education,* September 7, 2001.

67   *Harvard saw a 33 percent jump:* Sean Gregory, "Time Out: Gauging the Value of a Gap Year Before College," *Time,* September 21, 2010.

67   *Some 70 percent of women:* Bureau of Labor Statistics, U.S. Department of Labor, "National Longitudinal Survey of Youth 1997," http://www.bls.gov/nls/nlsy79.htm.

67   *girls are the better bet:* George Patrick Batten, "Patterns of Parental Spending: Do Parents Spend More Money on Sons or Daughters?" (master's thesis, Virginia Polytechnic Institute, 2013).

68   *they take their studies more seriously:* Nina DePena Hoe, "Not All Types of Delay Are Equal: Postsecondary Delay in the U.S. and Taking a Gap Year" (Ph.D. diss., University of Pennsylvania, 2014).

71   *colleges encourage such deeper reflection:* National Survey of Student Engagement, *Bringing the Institution into Focus: Annual Results 2014,* Indiana University Center for Postsecondary Research, Bloomington, 2014, 31.

75   *one in five young people:* William Damon, *The Path to Purpose: How Young People Find Their Calling in Life* (New York: Free Press, 2008).

75   *one-third of students who take:* Goldie Blumenstyk, *American Higher Education in Crisis? What Everyone Needs to Know* (Oxford and New York: Oxford University Press, 2015).

76   *a campaign promise Bill Clinton made:* For a good history on AmeriCorps see Steven Waldman, *The Bill: How Legislation Really Becomes Law: A Case Study of the National Service Bill* (New York: Penguin, 1996).

76   *six hundred thousand people apply:* Stanley McChrystal, "Lincoln's Call to Service—and Ours," *Wall Street Journal,* May 29, 2013.

78   *"to compete within the system":* Beth McMurtrie, "The Rich Man's Dropout Club," *Chronicle of Higher Education,* February 8, 2015.

79   *"awesome opportunity to learn":* Quoted in ibid.

Chapter 4: Why a College's Location Matters

82   *"We are 30 minutes from a Starbucks":* Scott Jaschik, "Shocking Decision at Sweet Briar," *Inside Higher Ed,* March 4, 2015.

90   *50 percent of NYU's freshmen:* Ron Southwick, "Presidents of Columbia U. and NYU Announce Their Resignations," *Chronicle of Higher Education,* March 5, 2001.

91   *women in the incoming freshman class:* Josh Keller, "As Its Popular Chief Retires, U. of Southern California Eyes an Encore," *Chronicle of Higher Education,* March 7, 2010.

91   *"the university geographically":* Quoted in ibid.

92   *LinkedIn analyzed the skills:* Sohan Murthy, "Defining a City by Its Professional Skill Set with Data from LinkedIn," *LinkedIn Official Blog,* October 22, 2014, http://blog.linkedin.com/2014/10/22/defining-a-city-by-its-professional-skill-set-with-data-from-linkedin.

93   *James Rhodes promised a college:* Jeffrey J. Selingo, "Location, Location, Location. Urban Hot Spots Are the Place to Be," *Chronicle of Higher Education,* July 28, 2014.

93   *"Choices are driven":* Caroline M. Hoxby, "The Changing Selectivity of American Colleges," NBER Working Paper No. 15446, National Bureau of Economic Research, Cambridge, MA, October 2009.

94   *In 1970, major metropolitan areas:* Sabrina Tavernise, "A Gap in College Graduates Leaves Some Cities Behind," *New York Times,* May 30, 2012.

94   *in every one of the twenty largest U.S. cities:* Ira Harkavy and Harmon Zuckerman, "Eds and Meds: Cities' Hidden Assets," Brookings Institution, Washington, D.C., September 1999.

97   *a million recent college graduates:* Joe Cortright, *The Young and Restless and the Nation's Cities,* City Observatory, Portland, OR, October 2014.

97   *"places that attract talent":* Quoted in Claire Cain Miller, "Where Young College Graduates Are Choosing to Live," *New York Times,* October 20, 2014.

98   *Denver is the new place to be:* Cortright, *Young and Restless.*

98   *new graduates were willing to move:* Sohan Murthy, "Where LinkedIn Members Moved for Work After College," *LinkedIn Engineering Blog,* May 5, 2015, https://engineering.linkedin.com/economic-graph/where-linkedin-members-moved-work-after-college.

99   *"touch and feel":* David R. Bell, *Location Is (Still) Everything: The Surprising Influence of the Real World on How We Search, Shop, and Sell in the Virtual One* (Boston: New Harvest, 2014).

100   *students enrolled in at least one:* I. Elaine Allen and Jeff Seaman, *Going the Distance: Online Education in the United States, 2011,* Babson Survey Research Group, November 2011.

100 *By 2013, it ate up more:* Jeffrey J. Selingo, "Tuition Perks for Faculty Brats: A Cost Colleges Should Reconsider," *Chronicle of Higher Education,* October 21, 2013.

103–04 *$600 million mini-campus:* Allan Appel, "$600M Yale Expansion Gets Final OK," *New Haven Independent,* November 17, 2011.

Chapter 5: Hands-On Learning for a Career

108 *he jumped at the chance:* "Dr. Schneider, 67, Cincinnati Dean," *New York Times,* March 29, 1939.

108 *Eventually, he persuaded his colleagues:* M. B. Reilly, *The Ivory Tower and the Smokestack: 100 Years of Cooperative Education at the University of Cincinnati* (Cincinnati, OH: Emmis Books, 2006).

109 *they didn't really spread widely until the 1980s:* Meaghan Haire and Kristi Oloffson, "Interns," *Time,* July 30, 2009.

112 *50 percent of the interns:* Finding accurate data on how many internships lead to full-time jobs is difficult. Several groups survey employers on this question, but the results largely depend on the size of the employers studied since larger companies tend to hire more of their interns. Some of the best data on this question comes from the Collegiate Employment Research Institute at Michigan State University and its *Recruiting Trends* report briefs (http://www.ceri.msu.edu).

113 *peak recruitment time for internships:* "No Experience Necessary? The State of American Internships, 2015," Burning Glass Technologies, http://burning-glass.com/wp-content/uploads/2015_Internship_Report.pdf.

114 *LinkedIn analyzed the online profiles:* Sohan Murthy, "An Internship Can Lead to a Full-Time Job, but Your Industry Matters," *LinkedIn Official Blog,* August 21, 2014, http://blog.linkedin.com/2014/08/21/an-internship-can-lead-to-a-full-time-job-but-your-industry-matters.

116 *A 2014 Gallup survey:* Gallup, "Great Jobs, Great Lives: The 2014 Gallup-Purdue Index Report," 2014.

121 *traces the roots of eight successful start-ups:* Frank Bruni, *Where You Go Is Not Who You'll Be: An Antidote to the College Admissions Mania* (New York: Grand Central, 2015), 132.

128 *enhanced training opportunities for students:* James Rosenbaum, Caitlin Ahearn, Kelly Becker, and Janet Rosenbaum, *The New Forgotten Half and Research Directions to Support Them,* William. T. Grant Foundation, New York, January 2015.

128 *52 percent of young people:* William C. Symonds, Robert Schwartz, and Ronald F. Ferguson, *Pathways to Prosperity: Meeting the Challenges of Preparing Young Americans for the 21st Century,* Pathways to Prosperity

Project, Harvard Graduate School of Education, Cambridge, MA, 2011.

129 *apprenticeships as a highly respected pathway:* Tamar Jacoby, "Why Germany Is So Much Better at Training Its Workers," *Atlantic,* October 16, 2014.

130 *a quarter of Swiss students:* Nancy Hoffman and Robert Schwartz, *Gold Standard: The Swiss Vocational Education and Training System,* National Center on Education and the Economy, Washington, D.C., 2015.

131 *"Apprenticeship is the other college":* Interviewed by Steve Roberts on "A New Push for Apprenticeship as a Path to Employment," *The Diane Rehm Show,* WAMU, July 28, 2015, https://thedianerehmshow.org/shows/2015-07-28/a-new-push-for-apprenticeship-as-a-path-to-employment.

131 *Apprentice School in Newport News, Virginia:* Nelson D. Schwartz, "A New Look at Apprenticeships as a Path to the Middle Class," *New York Times,* July 13, 2015.

134 *usually called "makerspaces":* Scott Carlson, "The 'Maker Movement' Goes to College," *Chronicle of Higher Education,* April 20, 2015.

136 *Occupations that require strong social skills:* David J. Deming, "The Growing Importance of Social Skills in the Labor Market," NBER Working Paper No. 21473, National Bureau of Education Research, Cambridge, MA, August 2015.

137 *cultivating your weak ties:* Mark S. Granovetter, "The Strength of Weak Ties," *American Journal of Sociology* 78, no. 6 (May 1973): 1360–80.

Chapter 6: Learning to Launch

142 *40 percent of the $1.19 trillion:* Josh Mitchell, "Grad-School Loan Binge Fans Debt Worries," *Wall Street Journal,* August 18, 2015.

150 *1,400 programs were under scrutiny:* Paul Fain, "Gainful Employment Arrives," *Inside Higher Ed,* October 30, 2014.

151 *earning less than $25,000 a decade:* Author analysis of U.S. Department of Education's College Scorecard, http://collegescorecard.ed.gov.

151 *employee training by some 15 percent:* ATD Research, *State of the Industry,* Association for Talent Development, Alexandria, VA, November 2014.

151 *"somewhere just below parking":* Susan Dominus, "How to Get a Job with a Philosophy Degree," *New York Times,* September 13, 2013.

153 *Half of the graduates of Harvard and Penn:* William Deresiewicz, *Excellent Sheep: The Miseducation of the American Elite and the Way to a Meaningful Life* (New York: Free Press, 2014).

155 *firms with five-hundred-plus workers:* Andrew Yang, *Smart People Should Build Things: How to Restore Our Culture of Achievement, Build a Path for Entrepreneurs, and Create New Jobs in America* (New York: Harper-Collins, 2014).

156 *University of Maryland's president:* Beth McMurtrie, "Now Everyone's an Entrepreneur," *Chronicle of Higher Education,* April 20, 2015.

160 *40 percent of VFA fellows:* Hannah Seligson, "No Six-Figure Pay, but Making a Difference," *New York Times,* July 13, 2013.

161 *20 percent today:* Teresa L. Morisi, "Youth Enrollment and Employment During the School Year," *Monthly Labor Review,* February 2008.

161 *students who are employed while in high school:* Donna S. Rothstein, "High School Employment and Youths' Academic Achievement," *Journal of Human Resources* 42, no. 1 (Winter 2007): 194–213.

162 *"From the moment I arrived":* Bruni, *Where You Go Is Not Who You'll Be,* 167.

Chapter 7: Redesigning the Bachelor's Degree

167 *Nearly 40 percent of American workers:* U.S. Census Bureau, "Current Population Survey: Educational Attainment," table PINC-03, 2014.

167 *Fifteen percent of mail carriers:* Carl L. Bankston III, "The Mass Production of Credentials: Subsidies and the Rise of the Higher Education Industry," *Independent Review* 15, no. 3 (Winter 2011): 325–49; Richard K. Vedder, "End U.S. Student Loans, Don't Make Them Cheaper," *Bloomberg,* June 17, 2012.

169 *a typical large university offered:* Burton R. Clark, *Places of Inquiry: Research and Advanced Education in Modern Universities* (Berkeley: University of California Press, 1995), 148.

169 *grew by 20 percent:* Jeffrey J. Selingo, *College (Un)bound: The Future of Higher Education and What It Means for Students* (Boston: Houghton Mifflin Harcourt, 2013).

170 *The first colleges in the American colonies:* The history of the curriculum in American higher education relies substantially on Arthur M. Cohen and Carrie B. Kisker, *The Shaping of American Higher Education: Emergence and Growth of the Contemporary System,* 2nd ed. (San Francisco, CA: Jossey-Bass, 2010).

172 *7 percent of new graduates:* Tamar Lewin, "As Interest Fades in the Humanities, Colleges Worry," *New York Times,* October 30, 2013.

172 *Just over half of students graduate:* National Center for Education Statistics, U.S. Department of Education, "Graduation Rates of First-

Time, Full-Time Bachelor's Degree–Seeking Students at 4–Year Post-secondary Institutions," table 326.10, 2013.

178   *four hundred thousand American students stray:* Selingo, *College (Un)bound.*

181   *Jimmy Iovine and Andre Young Academy:* The background on the USC program relies substantially on Jason Tanz, "Can Jimmy Iovine and Dr. Dre Save the Music Industry?" *Wired,* August 18, 2015.

182   *"a lot of it's cookie-cutter":* Josh Eells, "Dr. Dre and Jimmy Iovine's School for Innovation," *Wall Street Journal,* November 5, 2014.

184   *households earning $100,000 or more:* Sallie Mae and Ipsos Public Affairs, *How America Pays for College,* Sallie Mae, Newark, DE, 2014.

185   *11 million of them pay $50,000:* Carnevale, Hanson, and Gulish, *Failure to Launch.*

Chapter 8: Education, Delivered Just in Time

191   *"open loop university":* See http://www.stanford2025.com.

199   *less than 1 percent of undergraduates:* Mitchell, "Grad–School Loan Binge Fans Debt Worries."

199   *American students enrolling in graduate school:* U.S. Census Bureau, "Current Population Survey: School Enrollment," table 5, October 2013, http://www.census.gov/hhes/school/index.html.

200   *sixty-three coding boot camps:* Sarah Kessler, "Where Are the Women in Tech? Coding Bootcamps," *Fast Company,* August 24, 2015.

200   *MOOCs have attracted criticism:* Jeffrey J. Selingo, *MOOC U: Who Is Getting the Most out of Online Education and Why* (New York: Simon & Schuster, 2014).

201   *The web is full of DIY education sites:* Jeffrey J. Selingo, "To Reach the New Market for Education, Colleges Have Some Learning to Do," *Chronicle of Higher Education,* March 24, 2014.

203   *Employers spend $413 billion:* Anthony P. Carnevale, Jeff Strohl, and Artem Gulish, *College Is Just the Beginning: Employers' Role in the $1.1 Trillion Postsecondary Education and Training System,* Center on Education and the Workforce, Washington, D.C., 2015.

210   *LinkedIn announced it was buying:* Michael J. de la Merced and Mike Isaac, "LinkedIn to Buy Lynda.com, an Online Learning Company," *New York Times,* April 9, 2015.

Chapter 9: How Employers Hire

214   *"hiring doesn't seem to be as big a priority":* Peter Cappelli, *Will College Pay Off? A Guide to the Most Important Financial Decision You Will Ever Make* (New York: PublicAffairs, 2015), 146.

214 *main way a school gets to the top of the list:* National Association of Colleges and Employers, *Recruiting Benchmarks Survey Report: Key Measures for University Recruiting,* Bethlehem, PA, October 2014, http://www.naceweb.org/uploadedFiles/Content/static-assets/downloads/executive-summary/2014-recruiting-benchmarks-survey-executive-summary.pdf.

216 *the* Wall Street Journal *asked recruiters:* Teri Evans, "Penn State Tops Recruiter Rankings," *Wall Street Journal,* September 13, 2010.

217 *"a minimum ticket to ride":* Quoted in Goldie Blumenstyk, "When a Degree Is Just the Beginning," *Chronicle of Higher Education,* September 14, 2015.

218 *40 percent of the class of 2014:* National Association of Colleges and Employers, *The College Class of 2014 Student Survey Report,* Bethlehem, PA, September 2014, http://www.naceweb.org/uploadedFiles/Content/static-assets/downloads/executive-summary/2014-student-survey-executive-summary.pdf.

220 *To get to that number:* Chronicle of Higher Education, *The Value Equation: Measuring and Communicating the Return on Investment of a College Degree,* Washington, D.C., 2015.

221 *rated* none *of the twenty-five thousand job seekers*: Cappelli, *Will College Pay Off?,* 149.

222 *unstructured conversations have been found:* Frank L. Schmidt and John E. Hunter, "The Validity and Utility of Selection Methods in Personnel Psychology: Practical and Theoretical Implications of 85 Years of Research Findings," *Psychological Bulletin* 124, no. 2 (1998): 262–74.

224 *"Polish consisted of":* Rivera, *Pedigree,* 172.

224 *less than five hours researching:* Eugene Burke and Tom Gibbs, *Driving New Success Strategies in Graduate Recruitment,* SHL Talent Measurement, Corporate Executive Board, Surrey, UK, 2014.

225 *4,500 companies have at least one employee:* Lorenzo Canlas and Will Gaker, "The Analytics of People Analytics," presentation at the Wharton People Analytics Conference, Philadelphia, PA, April 2015.

228 *As Don Peck first reported:* Don Peck, "They're Watching You at Work," *Atlantic,* December 2013.

230 *hiring managers regretted making offers:* Corporate Executive Board Human Resources, "One in Five Hires Are 'Bad' Hires," *CEB Blogs,* April 9, 2013, https://www.executiveboard.com/blogs/one-in-five-hires-are-bad-hires-2.

231 *LinkedIn's sprawling headquarters:* My reporting at LinkedIn's headquarters was originally published as "Finding a Career Track in LinkedIn Profiles," *New York Times,* July 31, 2015.

234   *the budget of their career offices:* Chronicle of Higher Education, *The Value Equation.*

Chapter 10: Telling Your Career Story

238   *"plumbed the person's story":* Rivera. *Pedigree,* 149.

240   *40 percent of our work time:* Daniel Pink, *To Sell Is Human: The Surprising Truth About Moving Others* (New York: Riverhead Books, 2012).

243   *22 percent of graduates:* Cappelli, *Will College Pay Off?*

INDEX

ABOUT THE AUTHOR

JEFFREY J. SELINGO has written about higher education for two decades. He is a regular contributor to the *Washington Post* and is the author of two previous books, *College (Un)bound* and *MOOC U*. He is the former editor of *The Chronicle of Higher Education*. His writing has been featured in the *New York Times*, *Wall Street Journal*, and Slate, and he has appeared on ABC, CNN, PBS, and NPR. He is a special adviser and professor of practice at Arizona State University and a visiting scholar at the Center for 21st Century Universities at the Georgia Institute of Technology. He lives with his family in Chevy Chase, Maryland.